ANTIQUITY UNLEASHED
ABY WARBURG, DÜRER AND MANTEGNA

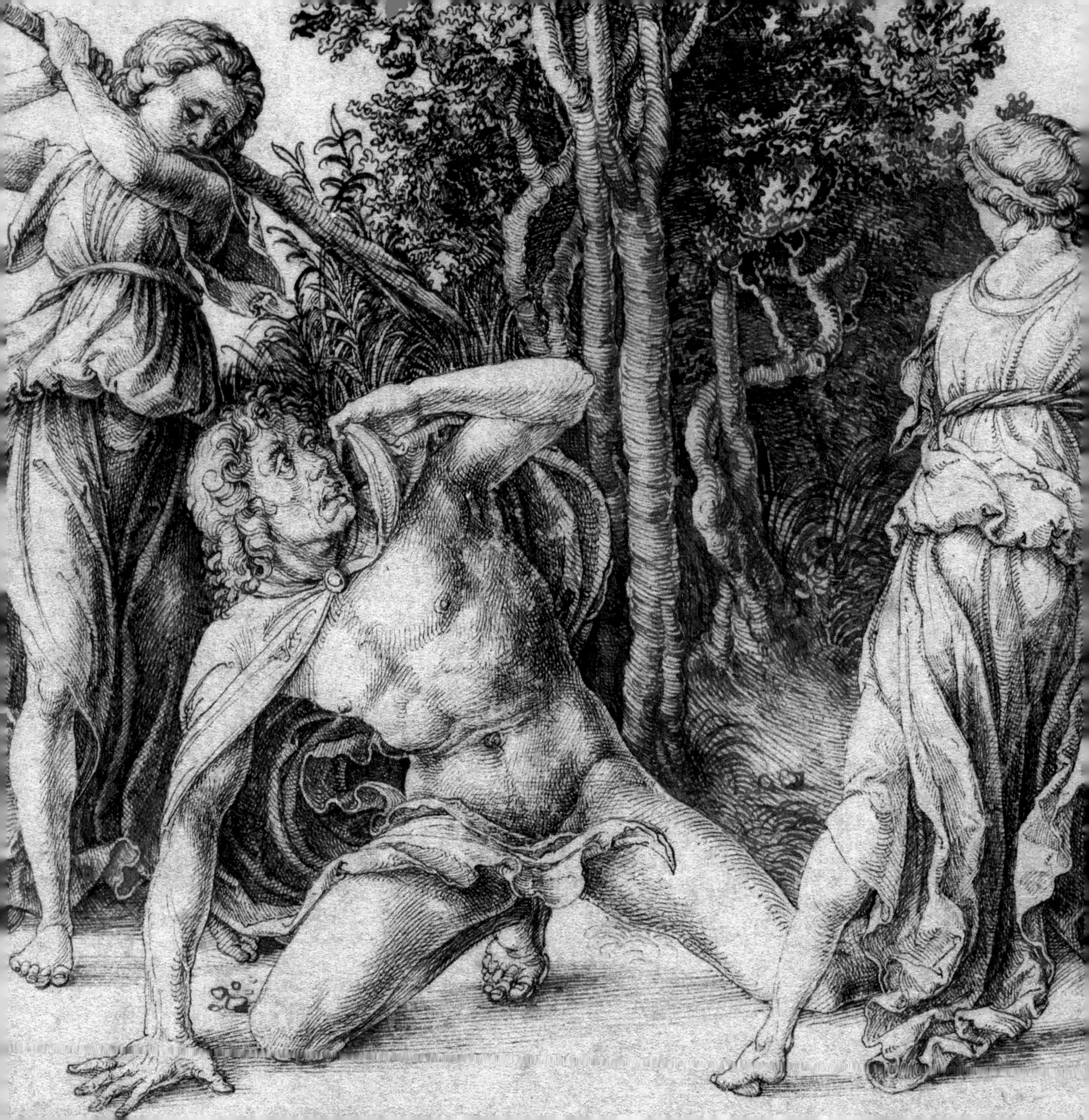

ANTIQUITY UNLEASHED
ABY WARBURG, DÜRER AND MANTEGNA

Marcus Andrew Hurttig

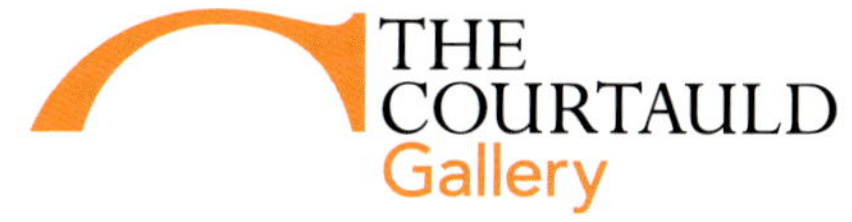

First published to accompany the exhibition

ANTIQUITY UNLEASHED
ABY WARBURG, DÜRER AND MANTEGNA

The Courtauld Gallery, London
17 October 2013 – 12 January 2014

ISBN 978 1 907372 58 2

British Library Cataloguing in Publication Data
A catalogue record for this book is available from the British Library

Edited by Stephanie Buck and Andreas Stolzenburg

Translations from the German by Kristin Lohse Belkin

Designed by Laura Parker
www.parkerinc.co.uk

Produced by Paul Holberton publishing
89 Borough High Street, London SE1 1NL
www.paul-holberton.net

Origination and printing by
E-graphic, Verona, Italy

The Courtauld Gallery is supported by the Higher
Education Funding Council for England (HEFCE)

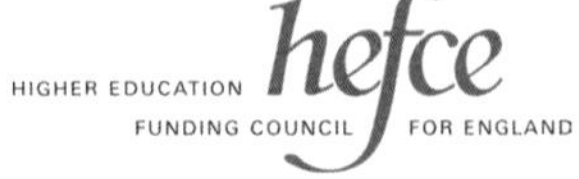

EXHIBITION SUPPORTERS
Embassy of the Federal Republic of Germany
International Music and Art Foundation

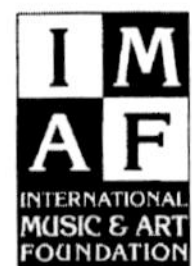

FRONT COVER Mantegna, *Battle of the sea-gods*, cat. 4 (detail)
FRONT FLAP Dürer, *Nemesis*, cat. 9 (detail)
BACK FLAP Dürer, *Melencolia I*, cat. 10 (detail)
PAGE 2 Dürer, *The Death of Orpheus*, cat. 1 (detail)
PAGES 10–11 Mantegna, *Battle of the sea-gods*, cat. 3 (detail)
PAGE 39 Mantegna, *Bacchanal with a wine press*, cat. 6 (detail)
PAGE 50 Dürer, *Ercules*, cat. 7 (detail)

INSIDE BACK FLAP Dürer, The Death of Orpheus, cat. 1 (detail)

CONTENTS

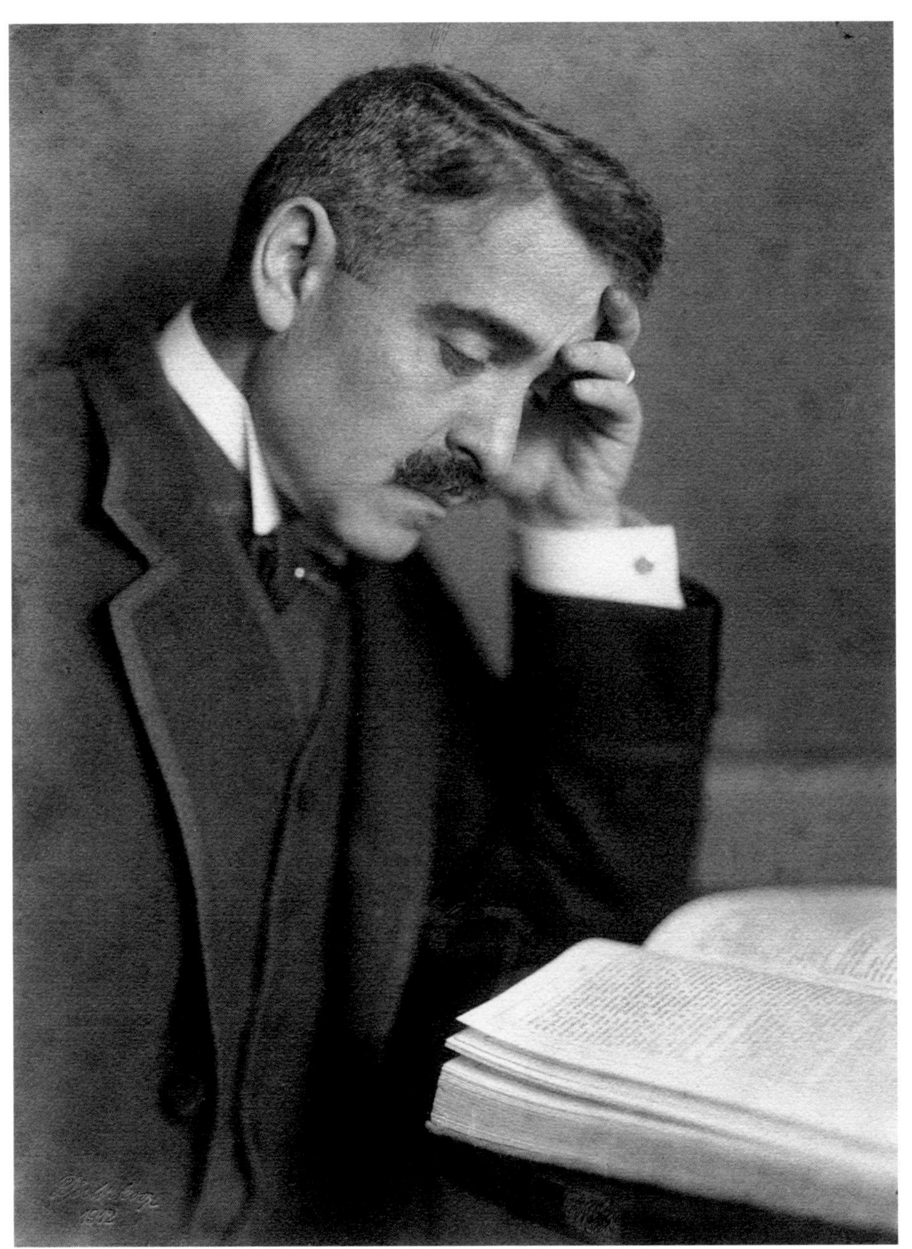

FOREWORD

Lord Lee of Fareham, who founded the Courtauld Institute of Art alongside Samuel Courtauld and Sir Robert Witt, recalled in his memoirs an incident in 1933 which may now be regarded as a turning point in the study of the history of art and culture in England:

> ... early in November [1933] ... I became so moved by the accounts ... of the impending fate, at the hands of the Nazis, of the famous 'Warburg Library and Institute' in Hamburg, that I took upon myself the responsibility of conniving at their surreptitious transfer to London .... Characteristic of Sam Courtauld ... [he offered] to subscribe £3,000 a year for three years, provided that his name did not appear in the matter. This noble stitch in time completely saved the situation and a few days later I received the glad but somewhat alarming tidings that the Library had got away from Hamburg and that the ship containing it was actually coming up the Thames.[1]

Aby Warburg, the sole founder and guiding spirit of this "famous ... Library and Institute" had died in October 1929 at the age of sixty-three in his home

town of Hamburg after having dedicated his life to the study of the legacy of classical antiquity in Western civilization. Not only was Warburg's German term '*Nachleben der Antike*' (literally 'after- life of antiquity') not easy to translate into English, but also his method of thinking was fundamentally new in a country where connoisseurship had a long tradition, but where the scholarly discipline of art history had only just begun to be taught at the Courtauld Institute of Art, founded in 1932.

Fritz Saxl, Warburg's former assistant and director of the Institute at the time of its escape to London, vividly described the challenge he and his colleagues faced:

> How could the six people who came over from Hamburg with the books set to work? The language in which they wrote – even if the words were English – was foreign because their habits of thought were un-English; and ... who would read what these few unknown foreigners produced? It was a strange adventure to be landed with some 60,000 books in the heart of London and to be told: 'Find friends and introduce them to your problems'.[2]

In London the Warburg Institute introduced itself through lectures, seminars and publications, but presented also several scholarly exhibitions (some of which were mounted in the Courtauld Institute). These drew upon the extensive photographic collection of the Warburg Institute, further developing ideas from Aby Warburg's final project, an 'Atlas' entitled *Mnemosyne*, a large series of images mounted on boards, which summarized Warburg's understanding of the forces that had determined the development of the Western mind.

The deeply visual nature of Warburg's arguments was already apparent in 1905, when he first introduced a larger audience to a central focus of his work, encapsulated in the term '*Pathosformel*' ('pathos formula'), referring to classical formulas for the representation of human passions adopted in Renaissance art. In a lecture given that year in the Konzerthaus in Hamburg, focusing on Albrecht Dürer's early drawing *The Death of Orpheus*, Warburg outlined his thoughts in the presence of the drawing itself, which he had borrowed from the rich holdings of the Hamburger Kunsthalle. This drawing, pivotal in the young artist's development as an ambitious response to classical antiquity, was displayed during the lecture alongside a group of engravings and woodcuts which included not only some of Dürer's own seminal later prints, such as *Melencolia I*, but also engravings by Andrea Mantegna which Dürer had copied in 1494, the same year he drew *The Death of Orpheus*.

Warburg's 'pop-up' exhibition has here been reconstructed. First developed by the Hamburger Kunsthalle in 2011, subsequently on view in Cologne in the Wallraf-Richartz Museum and now at The Courtauld Gallery, the installation has been developed by each institution slightly differently, while retaining the core group of works. In London, profiting from the Courtauld's long-standing partnership with its sister institute, additional documents from the Warburg archives have been included, while focusing also on Dürer's dialogue with Italy. This seemed particularly meaningful as *Antiquity Unleashed: Aby Warburg, Dürer and Mantegna* coincides and supplements the Courtauld's exhibition *The Young Dürer. Drawing the Figure*, which displays the figural drawings and prints which the artist executed during his travel years from around 1490 to 1496.

We are most grateful to Hubertus Gaßner, Director of the Hamburger Kunsthalle, and Ernst Vegelin van Claerbergen, Head of The Courtauld Gallery, for their keen and unconditional support of this project. The staff of both institutions embraced it with real excitement and we sincerely thank all involved, particularly our registrars Ursula Sdunnus and Julia Blanks and the Kunsthalle's paper conservator Sabine Zorn, who prepared the works for travel.

The collaboration with the Warburg Institute, London, could not have been more enjoyable: we are particularly grateful to its director, Peter Mack, for granting the loan of the original documents, and to Claudia Wedepohl for discussing all research questions.

Our special thanks are due to the author of this catalogue, Marcus Andrew Hurttig, who first conceived the exhibition in the Hamburger Kunsthalle in 2011 and remained wonderfully engaged throughout the realisation of the London venue whilst taking on his new curatorial role in the Department of Prints and Drawings of the Museum der bildenden Künste in Leipzig.

Supported by The International Music and Art Foundation, the exhibition is part of the programme at The Courtauld Gallery which seeks to share fresh scholarly research on drawings with the public and to raise awareness for the varied roles of works on paper in the history of art and thought. With an ambitious series of publications on its drawings collection the Kupferstichkabinett of the Hamburger Kunsthalle shares the same commitment. We are proud that the German Embassy has honoured our international co-operation with its support.

On 18 August 1929, a few months before his death, Aby Warburg wrote in a letter to his friend Jean-Jacques Dwelshauvers, alias Mesnil, "Not until art history can show … that it sees the work of art in a few more dimensions than it has done so far will our activity again attract the interest of scholars and of the general public".

Aby Warburg aimed at unlocking the meaning of an art work by excavating its roots in its cultural context. By restaging his display of 1905 with Dürer's *Death of Orpheus* at its heart, our exhibition both presents some of the most skilful and ambitious works on paper ever produced and seeks to introduce Warburg's rich intellectual universe to a broader public, hoping thereby to offer simultaneously enjoyment and food for thought.

STEPHANIE BUCK
Martin Halusa Curator of Drawings
The Courtauld Gallery

ANDREAS STOLZENBURG
Head of the Kupferstichkabinett
Hamburger Kunsthalle

1 Lee of Fareham, *A Good Innings*, vol. 3, London, 1940, pp. 1380–81. The library arrived on 12 December 1933 and was packed in 531 boxes; see Eric M. Warburg, 'The Transfer of the Warburg Institute to England in 1933', in *The Warburg Institute Annual Report*, 1952–53, p. 15.

2 Saxl in Gombrich 1970, p. 337.

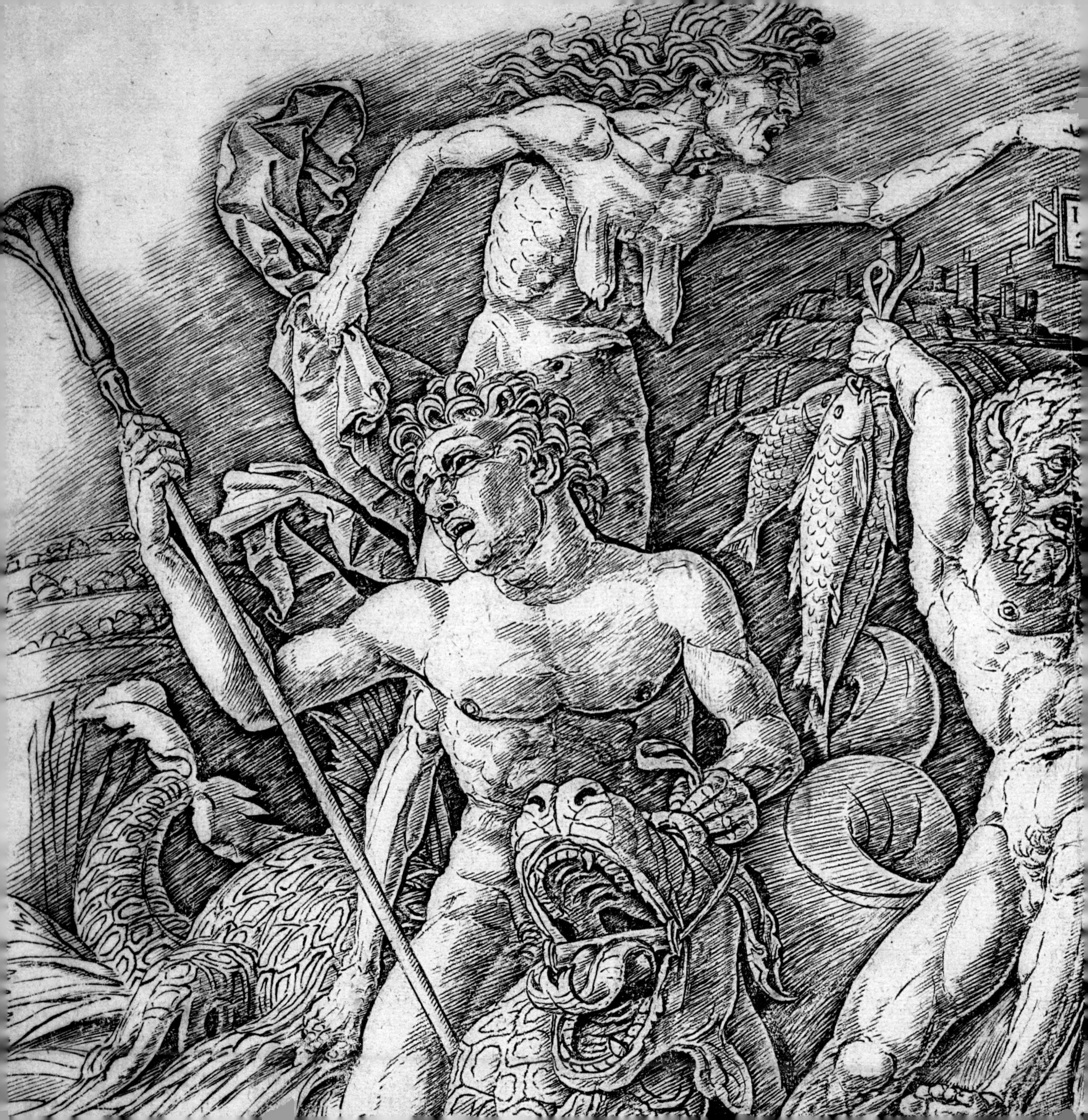

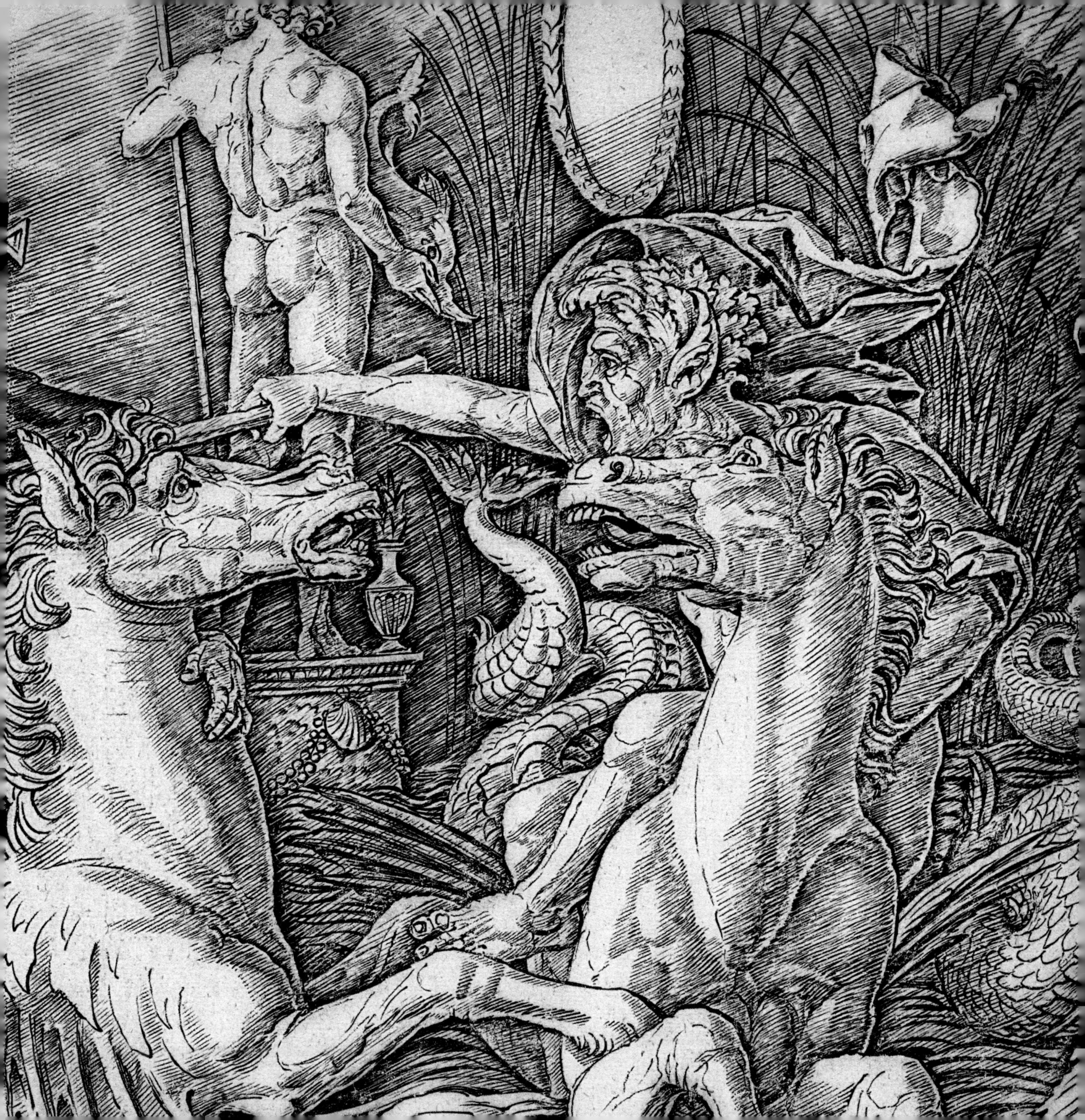

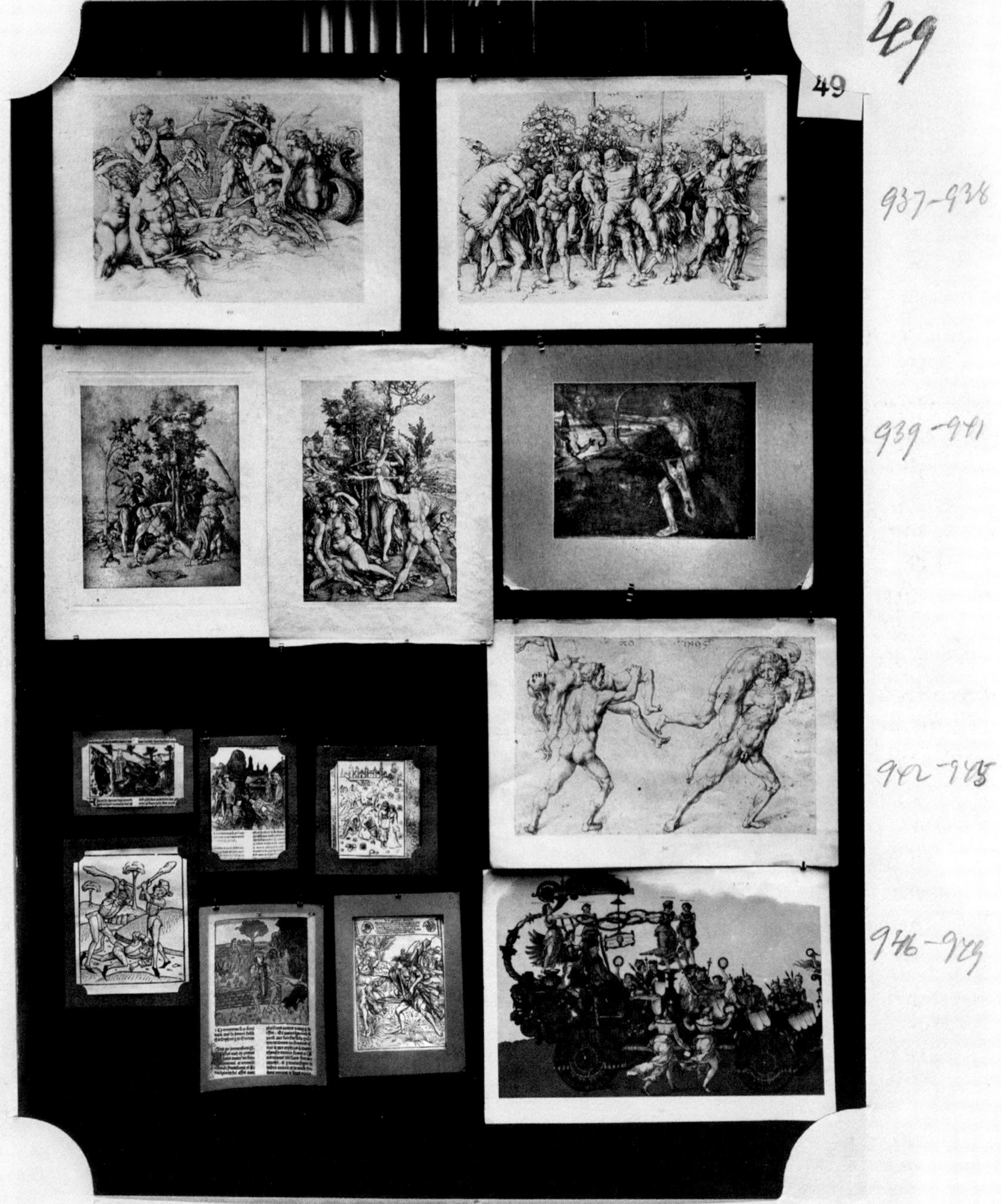

937-938

939-941

942-945

946-949

INTRODUCTION

The Hamburg banker's son Aby Warburg (1866–1929) was one of the most influential art historians and cultural theorists of the twentieth century. His life's work was devoted to tracing antique formulas in the representation of human passions in Renaissance art. For this epoch-spanning relationship, he developed the term 'pathos formula' (*Pathosformel*), first introduced by him in a lecture delivered at a congress in Hamburg in 1905. Warburg combined his lecture with an exhibition of prints and drawings to illustrate his idea of the pathos formula. That exhibition is here reconstructed and analysed.[1]

Warburg prepared his lecture for the Congress of German Philologists and Teachers (*Versammlung deutscher Philologen und Schulmänner*). Its conferences were attended by the most eminent German scholars from the natural sciences and humanities. In 1905 the conference took place in the Konzerthaus Hamburg (fig. 1) in the St. Pauli district from 3 to 6 October. Originally, Warburg planned to show the drawings and prints in the Department of Prints and Drawings in the Hamburger Kunsthalle and to deliver his lecture in the Konzerthaus afterwards. However, when

Aby Warburg, Image table 49 (Dürer) for his picture atlas
Mnemosyne, penultimate version, 2 September 1929
Warburg Institute Archive (doc. 5)

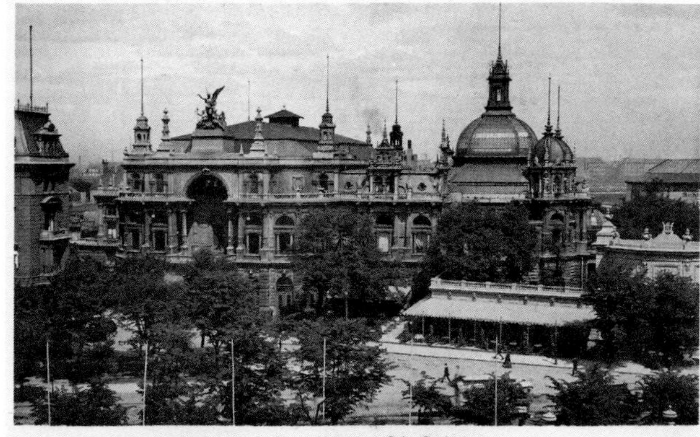

1 Konzerthaus Hamburg, run by the brothers Ludwig
Photograph by Wilhelm Dreesen, published in *Die Freie und Hansestadt Hamburg und ihre Umgebung*, Hamburg 1894
Hamburger Kunsthalle, Bibliothek

this plan had to be abandoned because of the tight schedule, he asked the director of the Kunsthalle, Alfred Lichtwark, on 21 June for permission to exhibit one drawing and two prints in the Konzerthaus,[2] namely Albrecht Dürer's drawing *The Death of Orpheus* (see inside back flap), an anonymous Italian engraving of the same subject, of which the only known version is in the Kunsthalle, and the engraving *The Carnival dance* ('*The Sausage Woman*'), traditionally attributed to Francesco Squarcione (cat. 1–2, 11). By the end of September, however, Warburg must have revised his ideas for the exhibition after consultation with Lichtwark. Instead of these three sheets (doc. 1), he now wished to borrow nine works from the museum:[3] besides Dürer's *Orpheus* drawing and the anonymous *Orpheus* print, there were to be three further engravings and one woodcut by Dürer and three engravings by Andrea Mantegna (cat. 1–5, 7–10). In addition to this display, Warburg intended to illustrate his lecture with approximately 50 slides, and he could hardly have adhered to the 30 to 45 minutes assigned to him (fig. 2).

On 5 October Warburg delivered his lecture 'Dürer and Italian Antiquity' (*Dürer und die italienische Antike*) to an audience of more than 300, according to contemporary press reports.[4] At the outset he distributed as gifts to the members of the archaeological section three plates (doc. 2). The nearly fifty-page manuscript (Warburg Institute, London) has remained unpublished,[5] but a short summary appeared in 1906 and was included in the first volume of Warburg's collected works, published in 1932.[6] In his lecture, the thirty-nine-year-old Warburg for the first time took stock of his many years of intensive research, attempting to interconnect the numerous results of his studies of Renaissance culture under the heading 'the afterlife of classical antiquity' (*Nachleben der Antike*).

Remarkably, the manuscript primarily addresses Gymnasium (grammar school) humanities teachers, whom Warburg tried to convince that the textbooks for art classes conveyed a one-sided image of antiquity and the vitality of its influence since the fifteenth century. He suggested that alongside the still dominant aesthetic doctrine of "noble simplicity and calm grandeur" (*edle Einfalt und stille Größe*) of ancient art, advanced by the archaeologist Johann Joachim Winckelmann towards the end of the eighteenth century,[7] the ecstatic, Dionysiac element in Greco-Roman culture should also be acknowledged.[8]

Winckelmann's approach to classical art accompanied a change of direction from the later phase of Baroque art towards what is now called Neoclassicism, figureheading a paradigm shift in the reception of ancient sculpture and its reinterpretation in modern art in the second half of the eighteenth century. This Neoclassical approach came to dominate the nineteenth century. Few voices were raised against it, but in *The Birth of Tragedy from the Spirit of Music*, published in 1872, Friedrich Nietzsche, taking Greek tragedy as his starting point, opposed the Winckelmannian conception of classical art, which he called 'Apollinian', with the 'Dionysiac'. In his theory Apollo fulfilled the principle that constitutes form; and Nietzsche assigned to him the visual arts. Dionysus on the other hand represented the tendencies in music that dissolved form. According to Nietzsche, however, the two gods, instead of obliterating one other, complemented each other in the creation of art in an inevitable fraternal union (*Bruderbund*).[9]

Warburg tried to apply this new perception, which inevitably jarred with the normal nineteenth-century reception of antiquity, to art history.[10] He accepted as fundamental that the sculptures of classical antiquity could indeed possess "noble simplicity and calm grandeur", in accordance with the god Apollo, but claimed that the passionate and destructive menace of Dionysiac power should not be ignored. In order

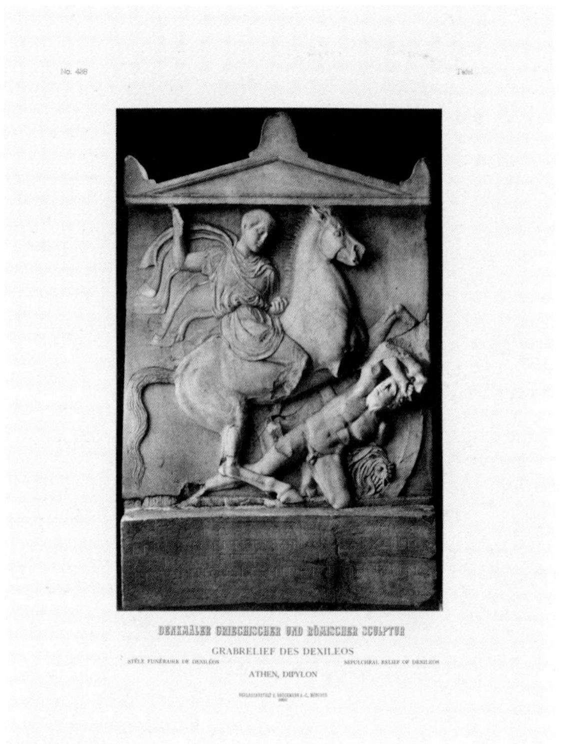
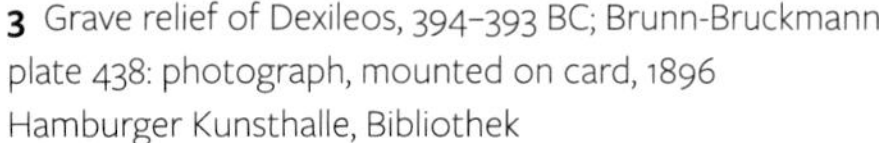

3 Grave relief of Dexileos, 394–393 BC; Brunn-Bruckmann plate 438: photograph, mounted on card, 1896
Hamburger Kunsthalle, Bibliothek

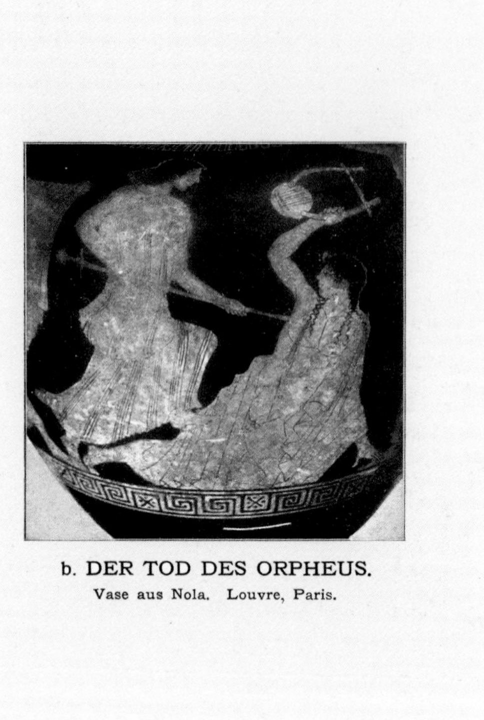

4 Detail from doc. 2, Plate I (Warburg's image series relating to the death of Orpheus), 1905
Hamburger Kunsthalle, Bibliothek

to investigate this complicated interaction, Warburg chose as his area of research the Early Renaissance, because he believed that artists such as Mantegna and Dürer had sought in ancient sculpture an image of man shaped by the passions. This was why he placed at the centre of his lecture Dürer's *Death of Orpheus,* thought to have been drawn in Venice in 1494 (cat. 1).[11] Warburg's opinion that Dürer's model

was an engraving by an anonymous North Italian master (cat. 2) was convincingly refuted by Joseph Meder as early as 1911–12.[12] Since then scholars have come to recognize that Dürer as well as the anonymous Italian engraver had, independently of each other, copied a lost work by Mantegna.[13]

The drawing's subject matter made it central to Warburg's research interests. Orpheus, after renouncing all love for women out of resentment for having lost his beloved Eurydice, and advocating instead the love of boys, placed his music in the service exclusively of the sun-god Apollo. As punishment, Dionysus, god of intoxication and ecstasy, sent maenads from his retinue who, in ecstatic rapture, tore Orpheus apart.[14] Such was its unembellished representation of the scene that until the end of the nineteenth century Dürer's drawing was generally thought to be a study after life.[15] This assessment was doubtlessly determined by academic art theory which, largely based on Winckelmann, could not envision such a passionate manner of expression in ancient art. Warburg was able to show decisively that Orpheus's defensive gesture was a faithful adoption of a motif going back to antiquity (figs. 3, 4), for which he coined the term 'pathos formula', which has since become in effect a technical term.[16]

Dürer experienced the art of classical antiquity through Andrea Mantegna and Antonio Pollaiuolo during his presumed first visit to Venice in 1494–95. Theirs was a very particular classicizing style that spoke to his own search for means with which to convey passion. Warburg pointed out that this Dionysiac approach in Dürer's early work contrasted with the perception predominant since Winckelmann that the form characteristic of the art of classical antiquity was Apollinian, representing man as serene and noble. The prevalence of this explains why the influence of classical antiquity in the work of Dürer had not been properly recognized in the nineteenth century.[17] For the four drawings that Dürer made after works by Mantegna and Pollaiuolo (cat. 1, 4, 5 and figs. 5, 6), which Warburg in his lecture called "pathos drawings" (*Pathosblätter*), ancient art had

hardly been considered as a possible model or basis. In contrast to Warburg's characterization of the *Orpheus* drawing as "filled with true antique spirit" (*vom echt antiken Geiste erfüllt*), Werner Weisbach coined, roughly at the same time, the phrase "fanciful classicizing" (*antikisierende Phantastik*).[18] In order to achieve an overview of the assimilation of the Greco-Roman pictorial world into the development of the arts in the Christian West, Warburg, from 1905 or earlier, drew up tabulated schemata.[19] Most of these sketches (doc. 3–4) show striking similarities with the photomontages of Warburg's picture atlas *Mnemosyne* (doc. 5; see p. 12). This monumental research project on the survival of antiquity, initiated by Warburg in 1926, remained unfinished at his death in 1929.[20]

The research concerning Dürer's relationship to classical antiquity and Italian art was linked to a further problem, once again essentially ideological. In German art-historical literature at the turn of the twentieth century Dürer's supposed two visits to Venice were generally assessed negatively, for nationalistic reasons. In the nineteenth century Dürer had been endowed with a national identity that served to legitimize the autonomy of Germanic culture and to counterbalance the hegemony of France and Italy in the arts. Inevitably, for this patriotic rhetoric, Dürer's dialogue with classical antiquity and the Italian Renaissance presented difficulties.[21] In this context, too, Warburg represented a more progressive point of view, when pleading in his lecture for the investigation of cultural exchange between North and South free of any national prejudice.

Dürer's *Death of Orpheus* was one of the pivotal works with which Warburg had been preoccupied since the 1890s. The high point in this context was

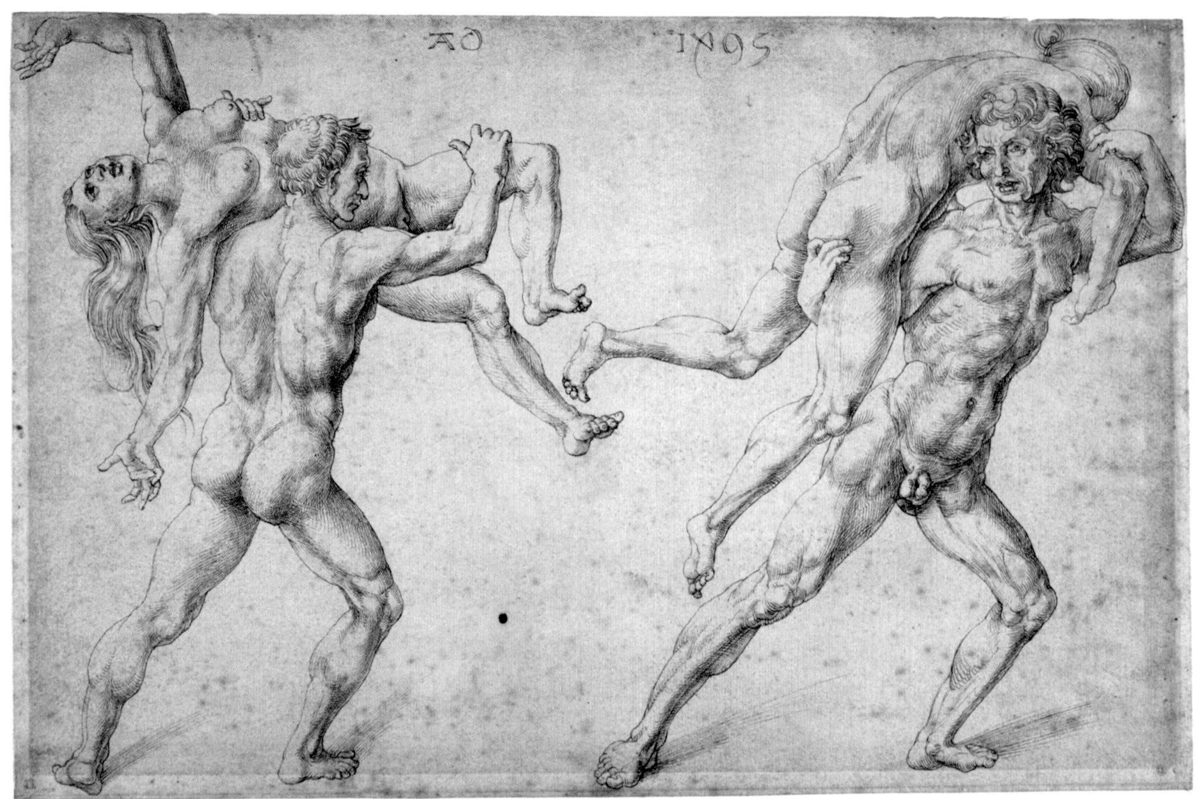

5 Albrecht Dürer, *Men abducting women*, 1495
Pen and ink, 283 x 423 mm
Bayonne, Musée Bonnat

undoubtedly his lecture 'Dürer and Italian Antiquity' (*Dürer und die italienische Antike*), the historiographic importance of which rests above all on the evidence it presented that the drawing was based on an antique representational formula. It was an important contribution to the study of formal relationships in art across the ages, and especially to the allure of classical antiquity for the early modern era. For Warburg, recognition of this formal connection constituted the starting point for further research into the survival and re-use of the Greco-Roman pantheon in modern times. This becomes especially evident if we consider that he saw Dürer's *Orpheus* drawing, together with a group of thematically related

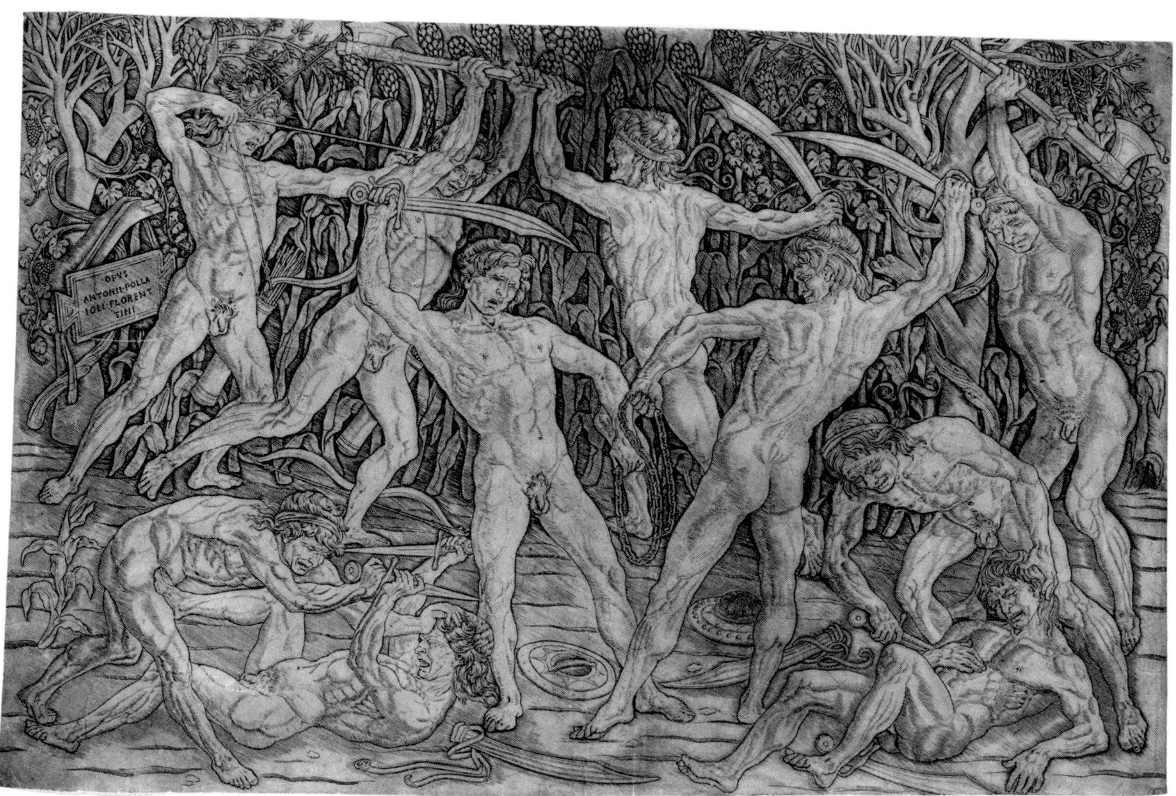

6 Antonio Pollaiuolo, *Battle of the nudes, c.* 1470–95
Engraving, 402 x 602 mm
Hamburger Kunsthalle

works (figs. 7, 8), as the immediate successors of the drama *Fabula di Orfeo* by the Italian Renaissance poet Angelo Poliziano (Politian; 1454–1494).[22] With this proposed relationship (which remains unproven), Warburg rigorously continued the Renaissance studies of the famous cultural historian Jacob Wilhelm Burckhardt.[23] For both scholars, the appearance of antique forms of representation in works of art constituted only a symptom of a process that affected all aspects of social life. They recognised that the Greek and Roman myths, of which a faint reflection had survived in popular medieval pageantry, entered with full force into Italian courtly life at the end of the fifteenth century.[24]

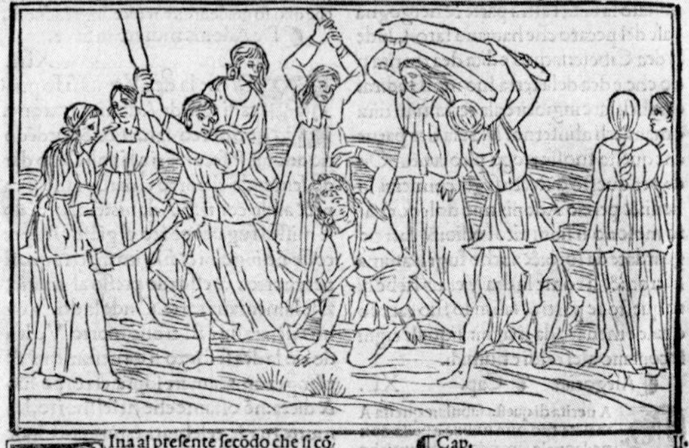

7 Unknown artist, *The Death of Orpheus*, woodcut, from
Ovid, *Methamorphoseos vulgare*, Venice 1501 (Book XI)
Hamburger Kunsthalle, Bibliothek

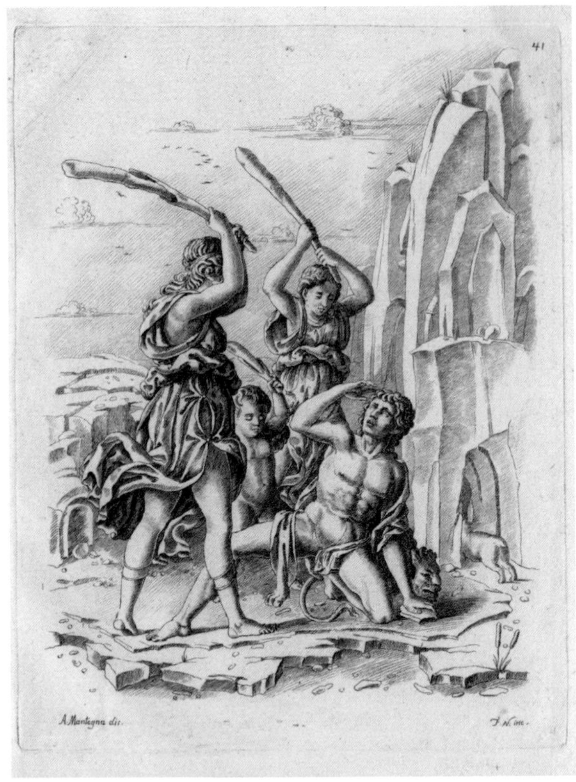

8 Francesco Novelli, *Scene of slaughter*, reproductive
print after a drawing by Marco Zoppo, published in
Disegni del Mantegna, Venice 1795
Hamburger Kunsthalle, Bibliothek

However, Warburg did not restrict the process of the revival of ancient, pagan cultural elements to the Renaissance. In the case of *The Death of Orpheus* he ignored all historical boundaries, endowing the subject with timeless, symbolic value. On 18 July 1905 he sketched out the following scheme in his diary: "Death of Orpheus – central myth of each faith: death of pagan divinity [as] counterpart and mirroring of the crucifixion" (*Tod d. Orpheus – Centralmysterium jedes Glaubens: der heidnische Gottestod Gegenstück und Widerspiel zur Kreuzigung*).[25] It is only with this expanded interpretation in mind that Warburg's criticism of Winckelmann's image of antiquity becomes wholly intelligible. Winckelmann believed that the "noble simplicity and calm grandeur" of antique statues reflected the lifestyle of ancient Greece.[26] Warburg critically opposed this idealistic view by affirming Nietzsche's Dionysiac principle that could at any time threaten the civilizing processes in the Western world.

Such a case occurred in Russia in early December 1905 when a horde of enraged Czarist soldiers brutally murdered a young female teacher because of her religious views. The article about this atrocity in the *Frankfurter Zeitung* reads like an inverted modern version of the Orpheus myth. Warburg recognized this and pasted the article at the end of his lecture manuscript with the warning: "The death of Orpheus. The return of the beast, for ever unchanged, called *homo sapiens*" (*Der Tod d. Orpheus. Die Rückkehr der ewig gleichen Bestie, gen. Homo Sapiens*) (fig. 9).[27]

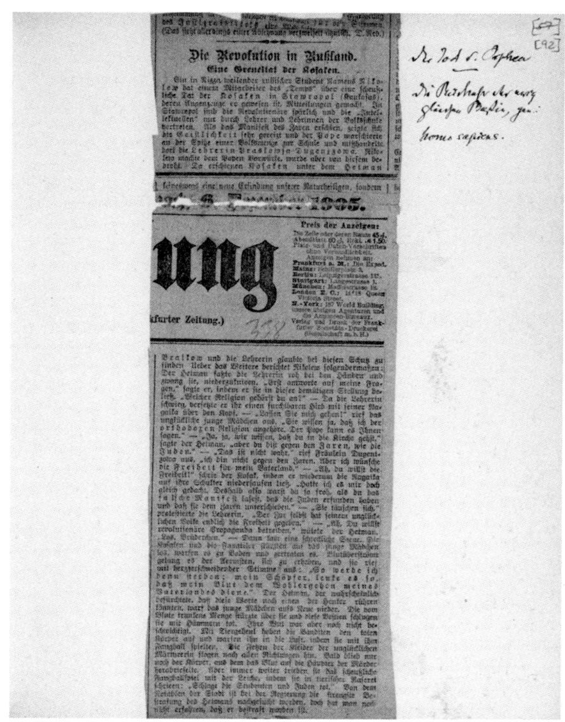

9 Aby Warburg, Newspaper attachment to the manuscript of his lecture 'Dürer and Italian Antiquity', 1905
London, Warburg Institute Archive

1 The exhibition was previously shown under the title *Die entfesselte Antike: Aby Warburg und die Geburt der Pathosformel* (*in Hamburg*) in the Kunsthalle, Hamburg (27 March – 26 June 2011) and the Wallraf-Richartz-Museum and Fondation Corboud, Cologne (1 March – 28 May 2012), each with a catalogue; see Hurttig 2011.

2 Cf. Warburg's letter to Lichtwark, 21 June 1905: Hamburger Kunsthalle, Archive, Direktorenkorrespondenz, no. 71; transcribed in Hurttig 2011, pp. 71–72 (letter 22).

3 Cf. Warburg's letter to Lichtwark, 16 September 1905: Hamburger Kunsthalle, Archive, Direktorenkorrespondenz, no. 73; copy in the Warburg Institute Archive, London [WIA]; transcribed in Hurttig 2011, p. 74 (letter 26).

4 See *Hamburger Nachrichten*, 5 October 1905, no. 701 (evening edition).

5 WIA, III.61.6.1. On the manuscript, see also Schoell-Glass 2008, pp. 45–49.

6 Warburg 1906, pp. 55–60; Warburg 1932/1998, pp. 443–50; further reprints in Warburg 1979, pp. 125–36; Warburg 2010, pp. 176–83. Two handwritten summaries of the lecture survive that vary slightly from the printed version: WIA, III.61.1. and III.61.2.

7 The famous phrase which Winckelmann formulated in connection with the Late Hellenistic sculpture *Laocoon* appears for the first time in the book *Gedanken über die Nachahmung der griechischen Werke in Malerei und Bildhauerkunst*, published in 1755; Winckelmann 1825–29, vol. 1, pp. 30–31; Winckelmann 1987, pp. 33, 35.

8 Warburg's critical response to Winckelmann can be traced back to his 1892–93 doctoral thesis on Botticelli: see Warburg 1932/1998, p. 55; Warburg 1979, p. 49; Warburg 2010, p. 108. This concern is especially expressed in his lecture of 1914, 'Der Eintritt des antikisierenden Idealstils in die Malerei der Frührenaissance': see Warburg 1932/1998, pp. 173–76; Warburg 2010, pp. 280–310. On Warburg and Winckelmann, see Didi-Huberman 2002, pp. 27–29 (with further literature).

9 Nietzsche [1999], vol. 1, pp. 62, 137, 140; Nietzsche [1964], vol. 1, pp. 68, 166–67, 180.

10 On Warburg and Nietzsche, see Didi-Huberman 2002, pp. 155–68.

11 For a summary of the extensive literature on Dürer's *Orpheus* drawing, see Prange 2007, vol. 1, pp. 146–48 ; for a discussion of Dürer's controversial first trip to Italy around 1494–95 see Ferrari 2007, pp. 45–49; Eser 2012, pp. 542–44; London 2013, pp. 31–32.

12 Meder 1911–12, p. 213.

13 Roesler-Friedenthal 1996, p. 151; Ekserdjian 1998, pp. 145–48.

14 On the literary tradition and iconography of the Orpheus myth, see Warden 1982; Schröter 2003, pp. 109–58.

15 Cf. Ephrussi 1882, pp. 24–25.

16 On the term 'pathos formula', see Gombrich 1970, p. 179, note 1; Hofmann/Syamken/Warnke 1980, pp. 53–83; Wind 1991, p. 73; Settis 1993, pp. 142–45, 150; Didi-Huberman 2002, pp. 22–23.

17 See Białostocki 1986, pp. 333–52.

18 Warburg 1906, p. 56; Weisbach 1906, p. 61.

19 WIA, III.61.1. Cf. Didi-Huberman 2002, p. 462.

20 Three versions of the picture atlas are documented: WIA III.105.1.1, III.105.2. and III.107.3. The presumably final, third version was published as accompanying material to the 1994 Warburg exhibition in Kunsthaus Hamburg and as vol. II. 1 in Warburg's collected works (Warburg 2000). On the creation and function of the picture atlas, see Hofmann/Syamken/Warnke 1980, p. 157; Warburg 2010, pp. 603–05.

21 On the reception of Dürer in the nineteenth century, see Białostocki 1986, pp. 222, 231–32, 309–32.

22 The play is thought to have been performed for the first time at the court in Mantua in 1480; see Pirrotta 1975, pp. 6ff.; Guthmüller 1986, pp. 71–73; Schröter 2003, p. 132.

23 On Burckhardt's influence on Warburg, see Warnke 1991, pp. 79–86; Didi-Huberman 2002, pp. 72–81.

24 Burckhardt 1860, pp. 400–26; Burckhardt 1990, pp. 256–70; Warburg 1932/1998, pp. 66–67; see Warburg 2010, p. 172.

25 Warburg's diary, 1 January 1903 to August 1914, fol. 36: WIA, III.10.3.

26 Winckelmann 1825–29, vol. 1, pp. 30–31; vol. 3, pp. 133–36; Winckelmann 2006, pp. 120–22.

27 WIA, III.61.6.1, fol. 92 (Frankfurter Zeitung, 6. 12. 1905, no. 338); Schoell-Glass 2008, pp. 50–51.

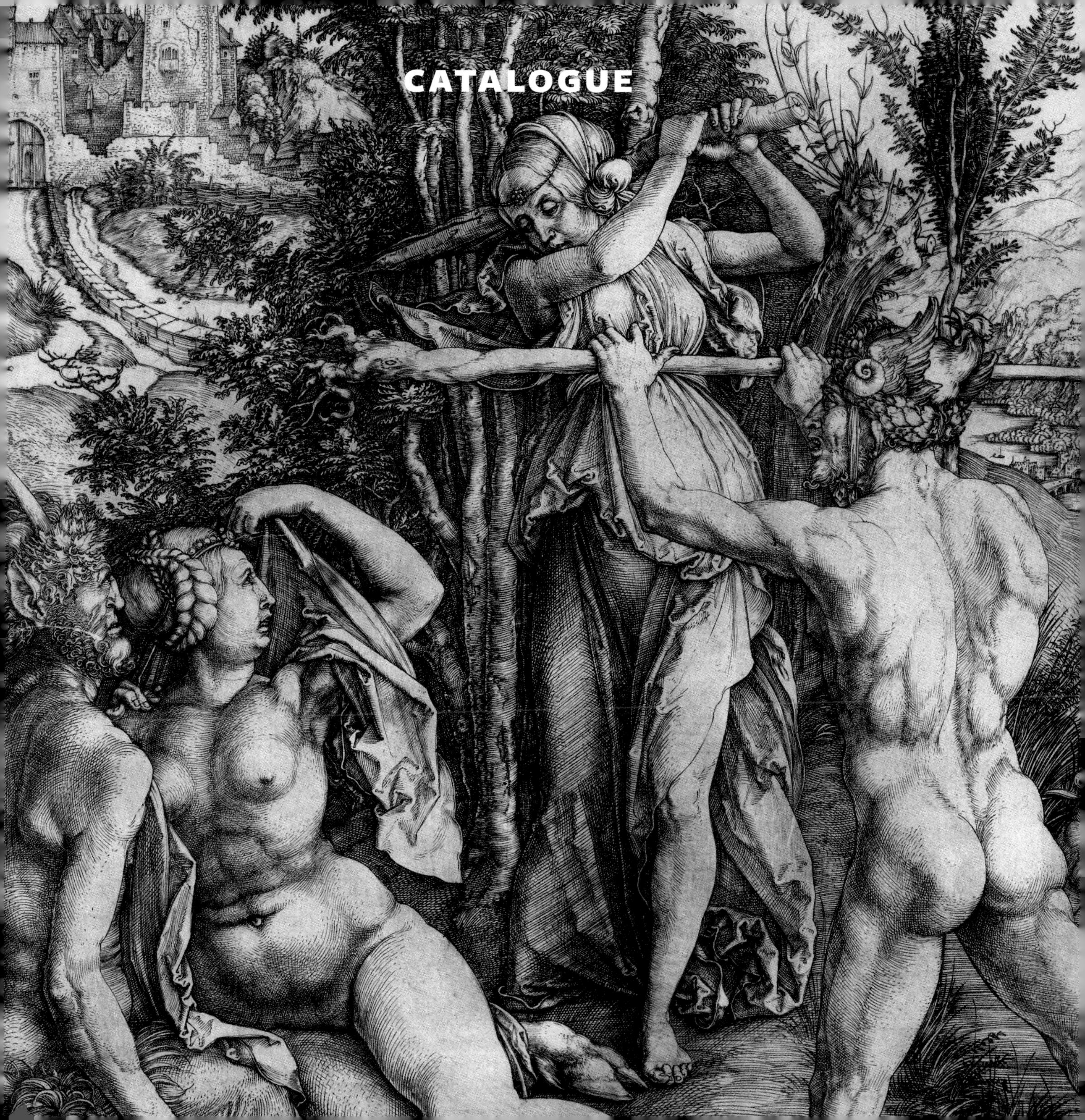
CATALOGUE

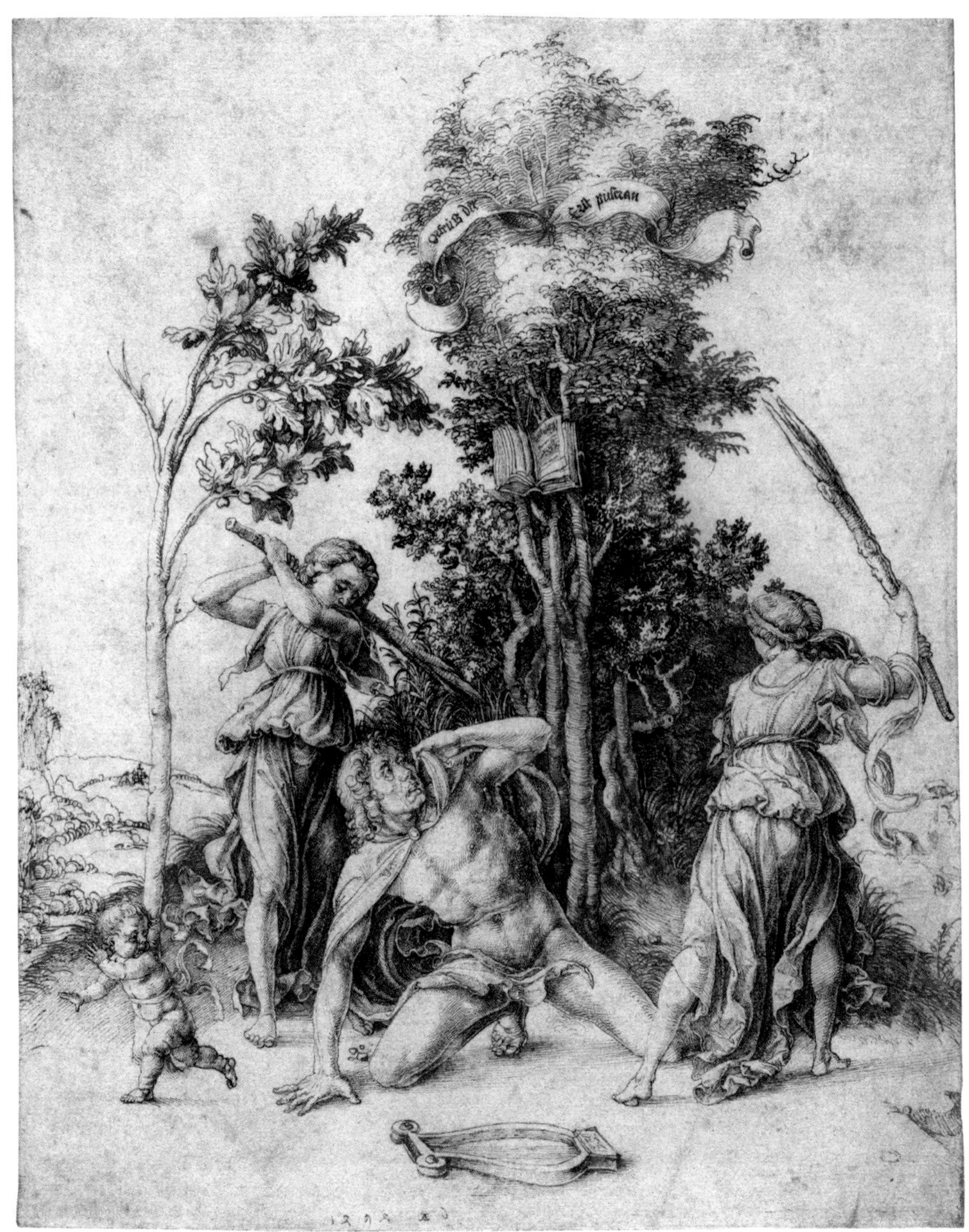

1

ALBRECHT DÜRER
The Death of Orpheus, 1494
Pen and brown ink, 289 x 225 mm

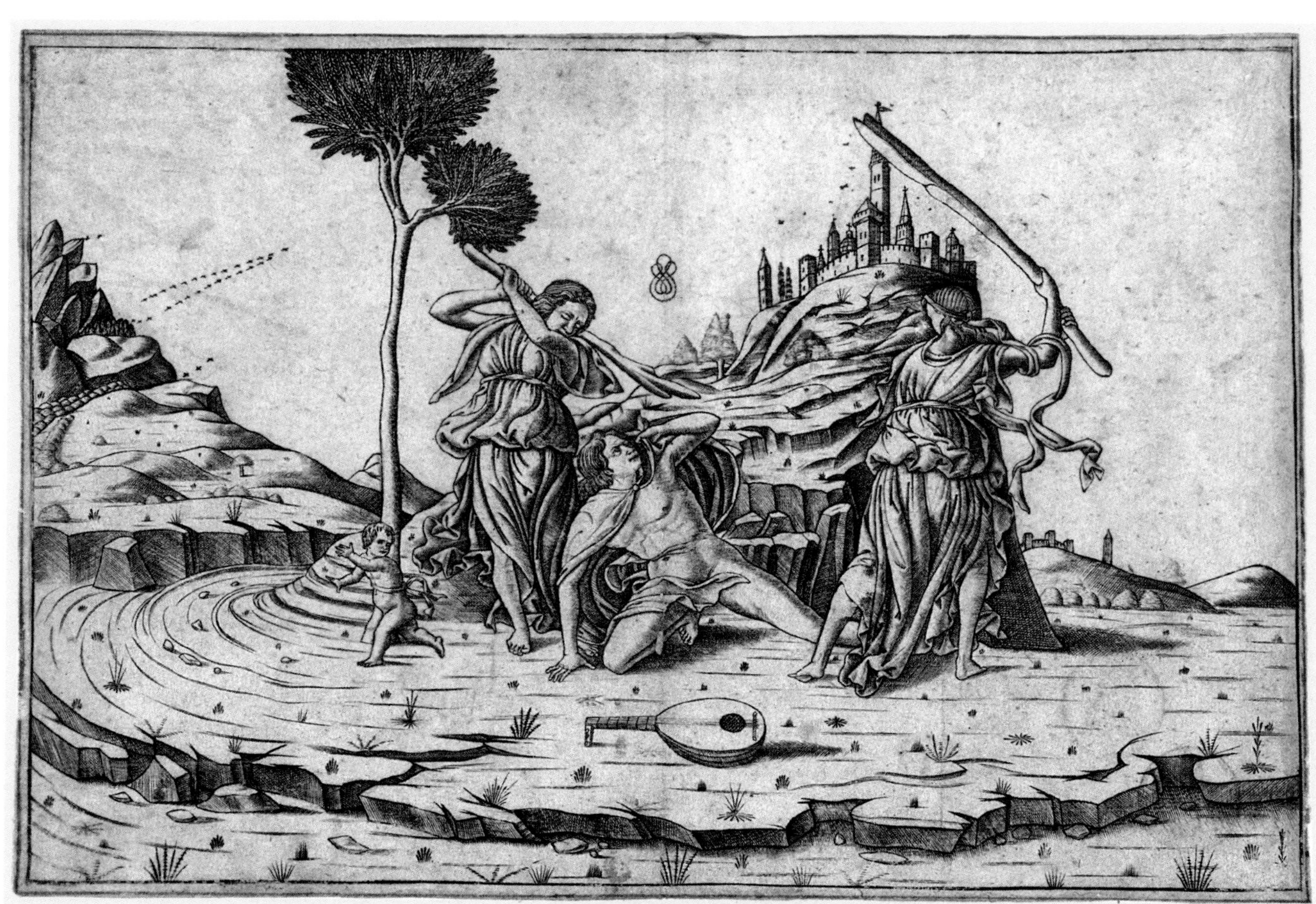

2

FERRARA

The Death of Orpheus, last third of 15th century

Engraving, 146 x 216 mm

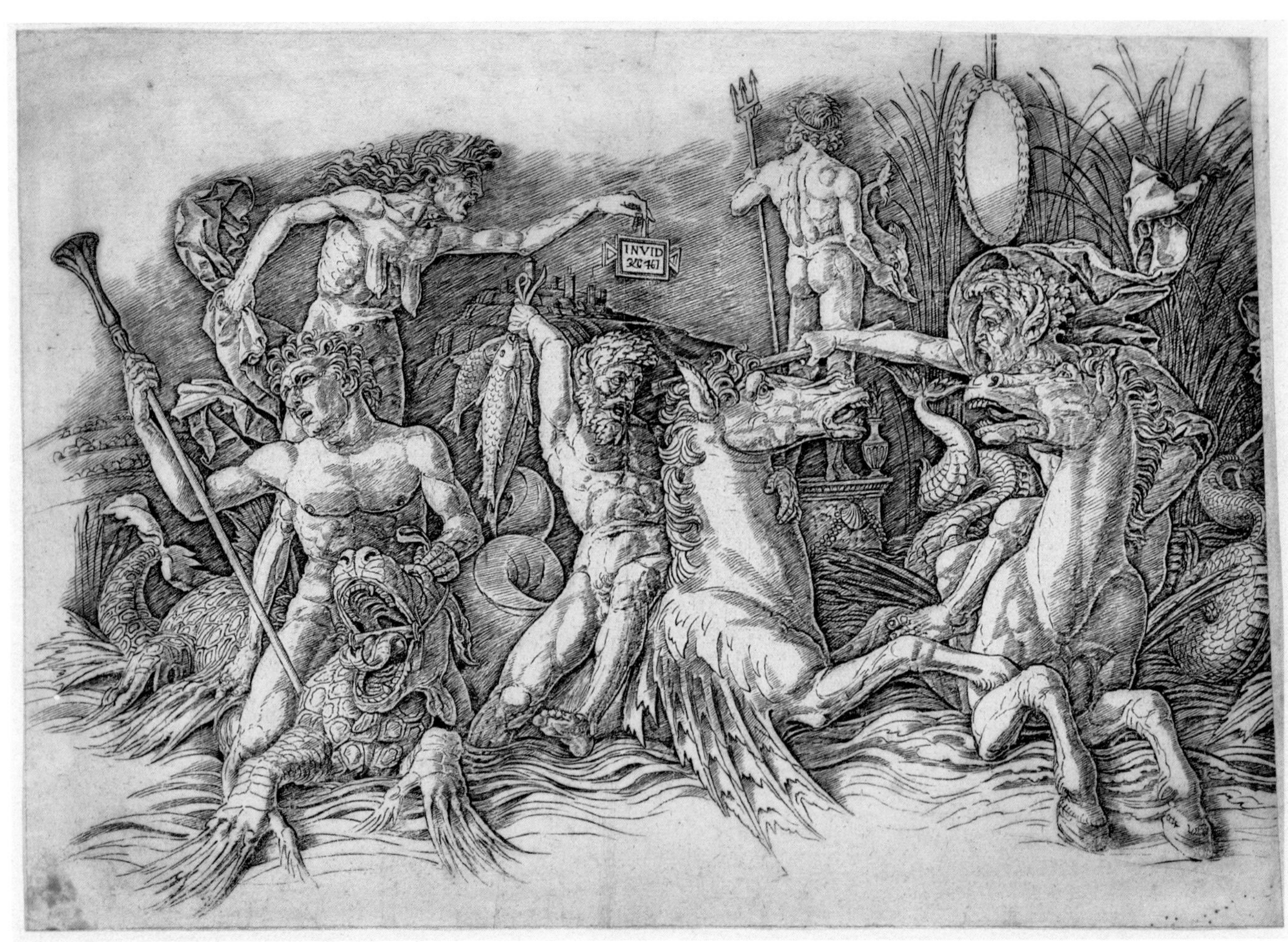

3

ANDREA MANTEGNA

Battle of the sea-gods (left half), c. 1475–80
Engraving and drypoint, 314 x 435 mm

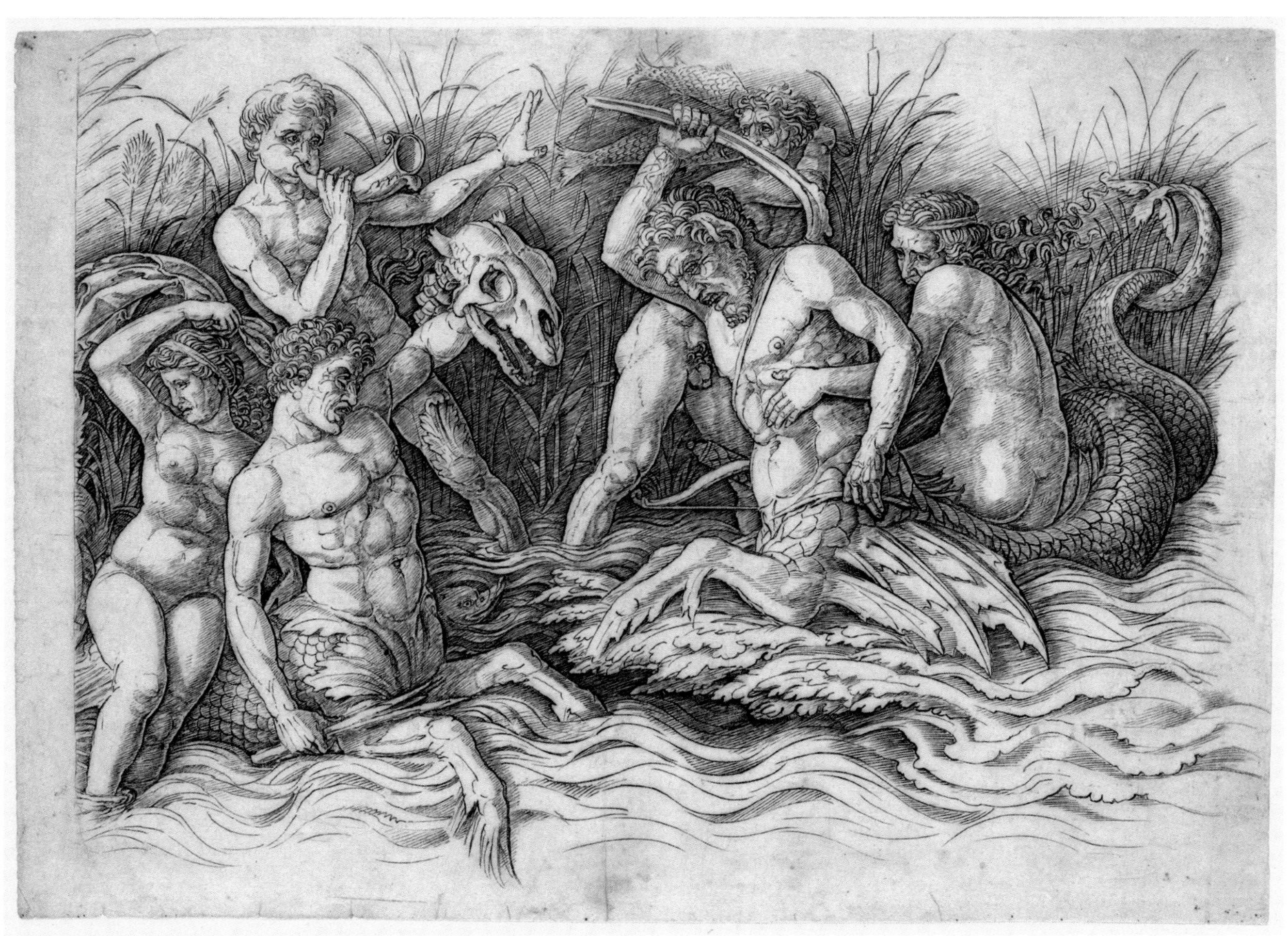

4

Battle of the sea-gods (right half), c. 1475–80
Engraving and drypoint, 305 x 442 mm

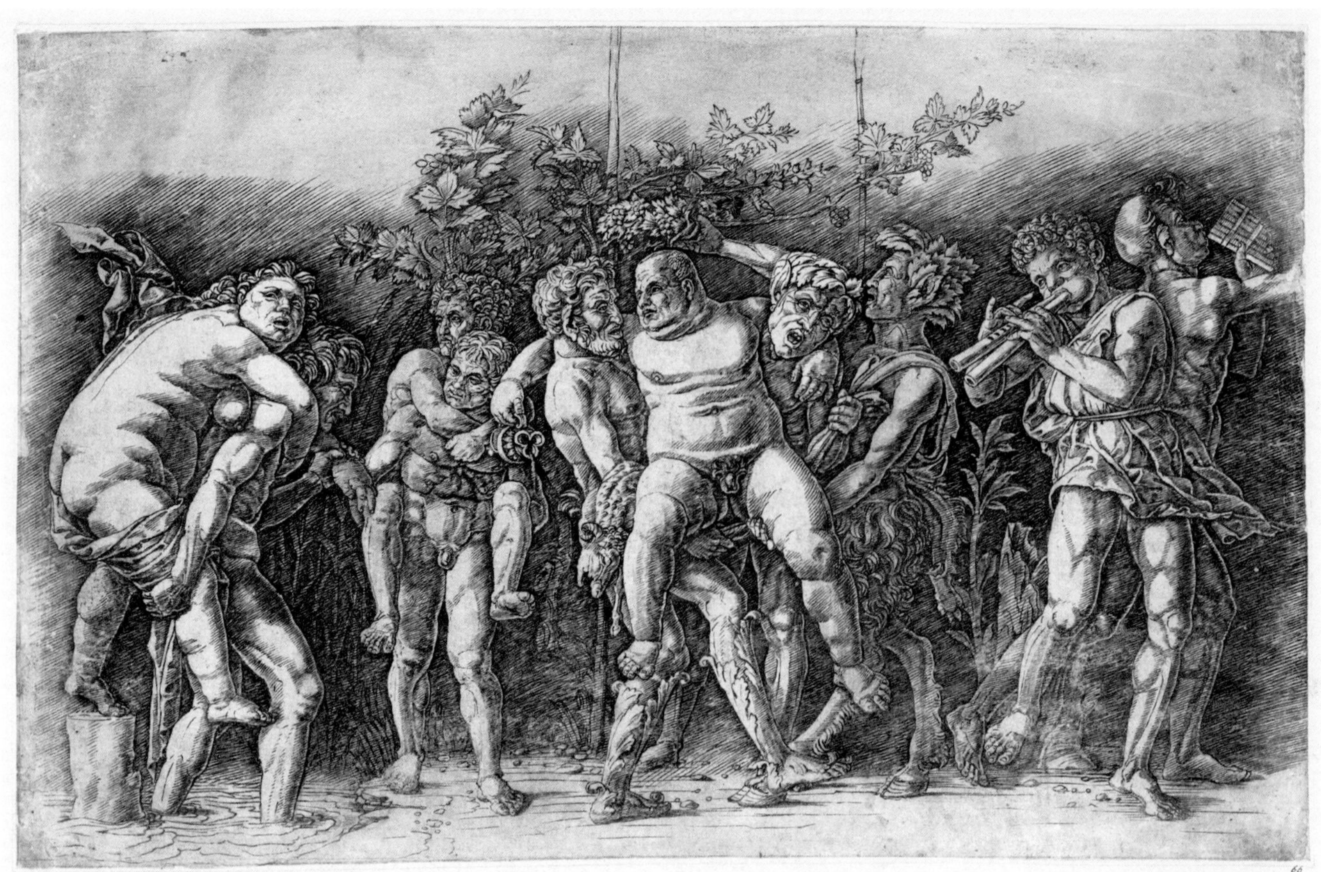

5

ANDREA MANTEGNA

Bacchanal with Silenus, c. 1475–80

Engraving and drypoint, 290 x 447 mm

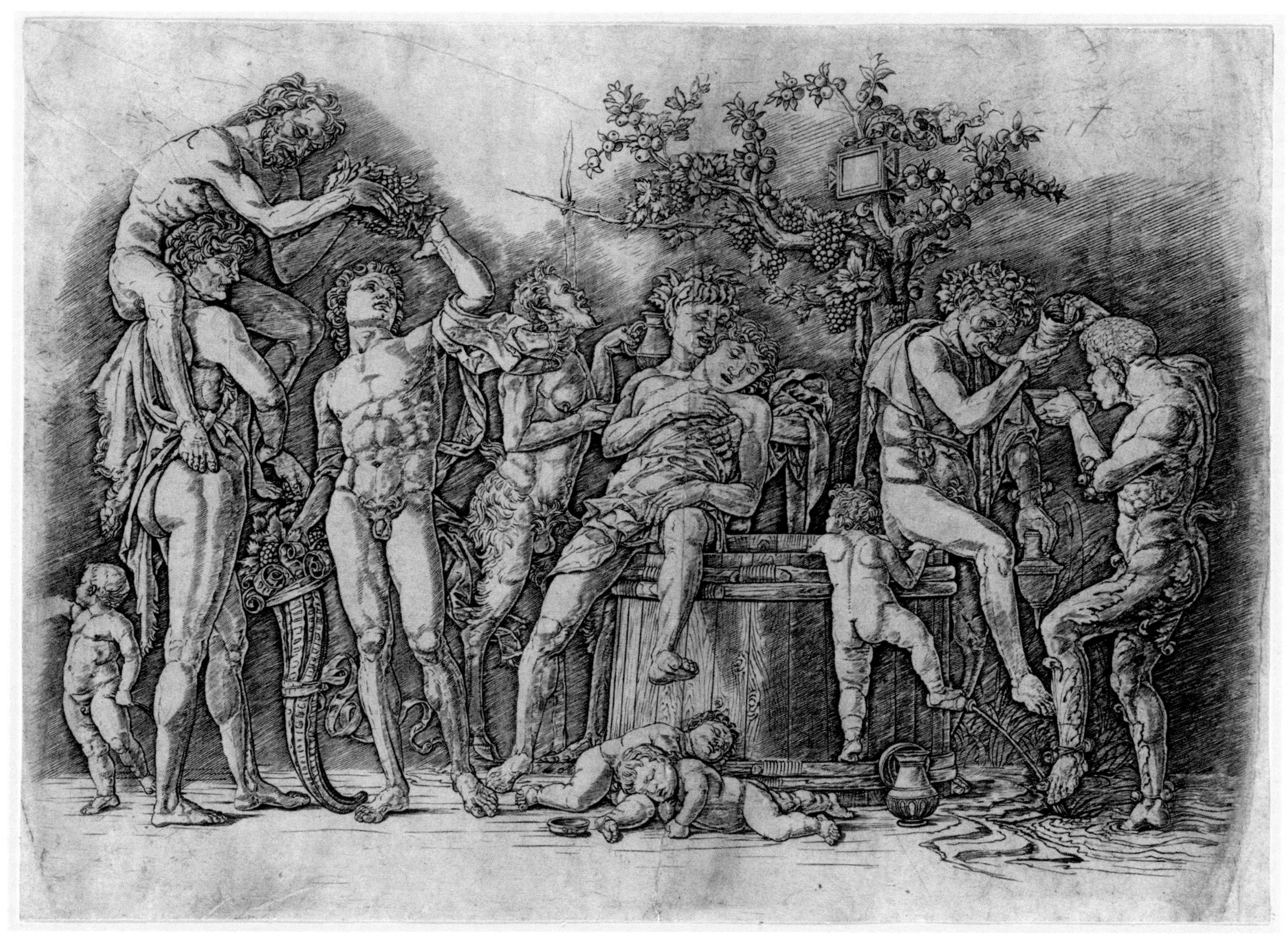

6

ANDREA MANTEGNA

Bacchanal with a wine press, c. 1475–80

Engraving and drypoint, 330 x 457 mm

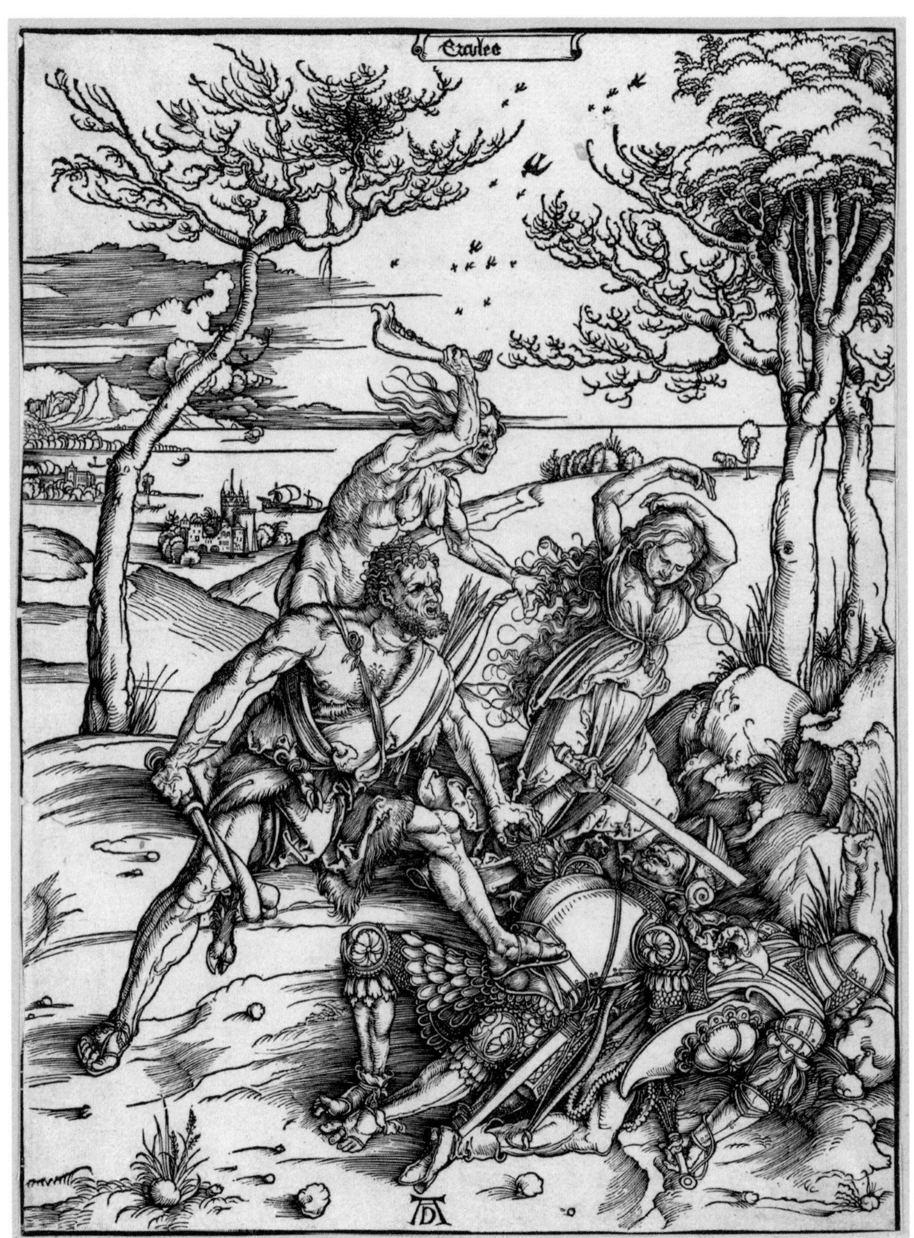

7

ALBRECHT DÜRER

Ercules (The Madness of Hercules), c. 1496
Woodcut, 390 x 283 mm (block)

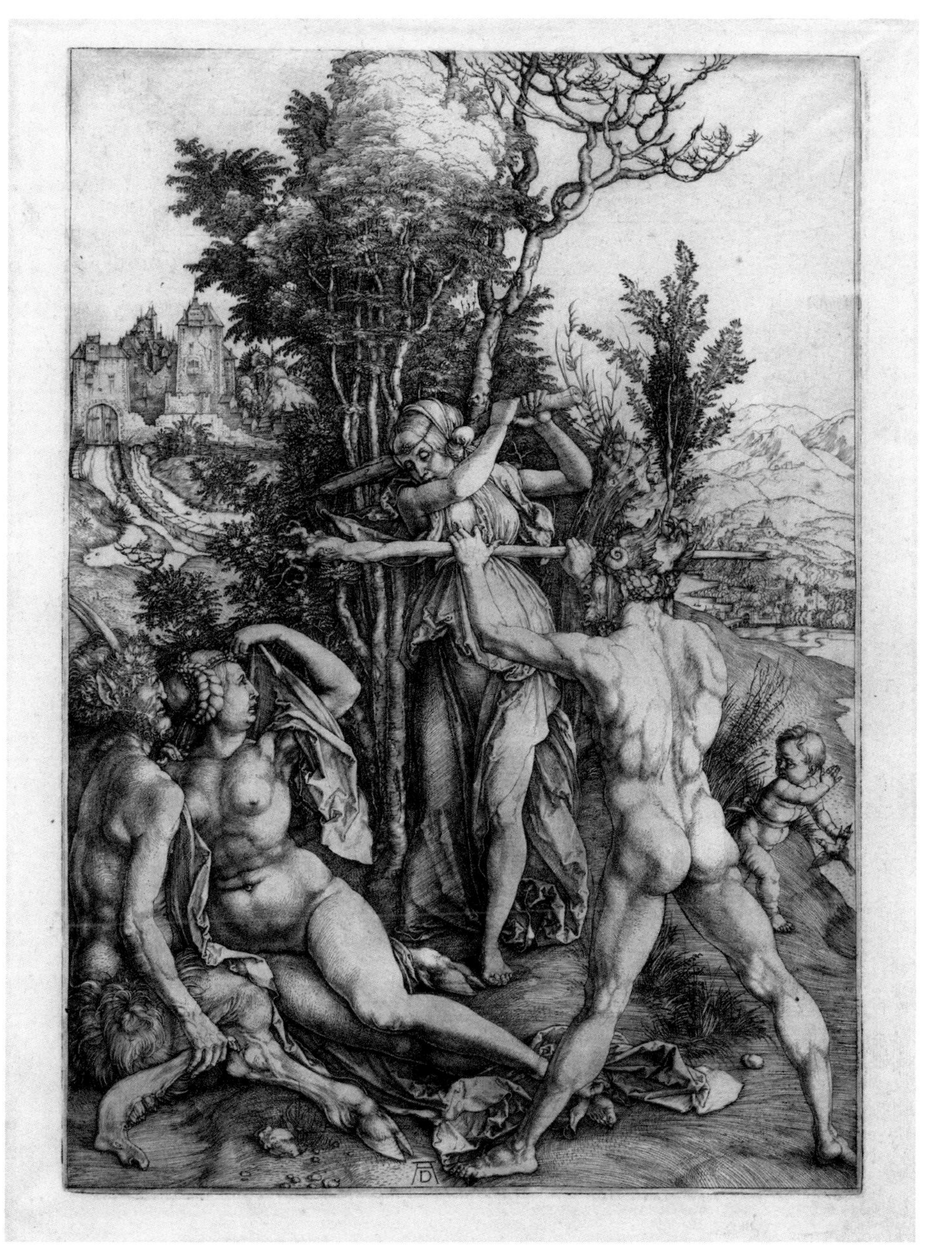

8

ALBRECHT DÜRER

Hercules at the Crossroads (Jealousy), c. 1498

Engraving, 352 x 262 mm (sheet), 323 x 223 mm (plate)

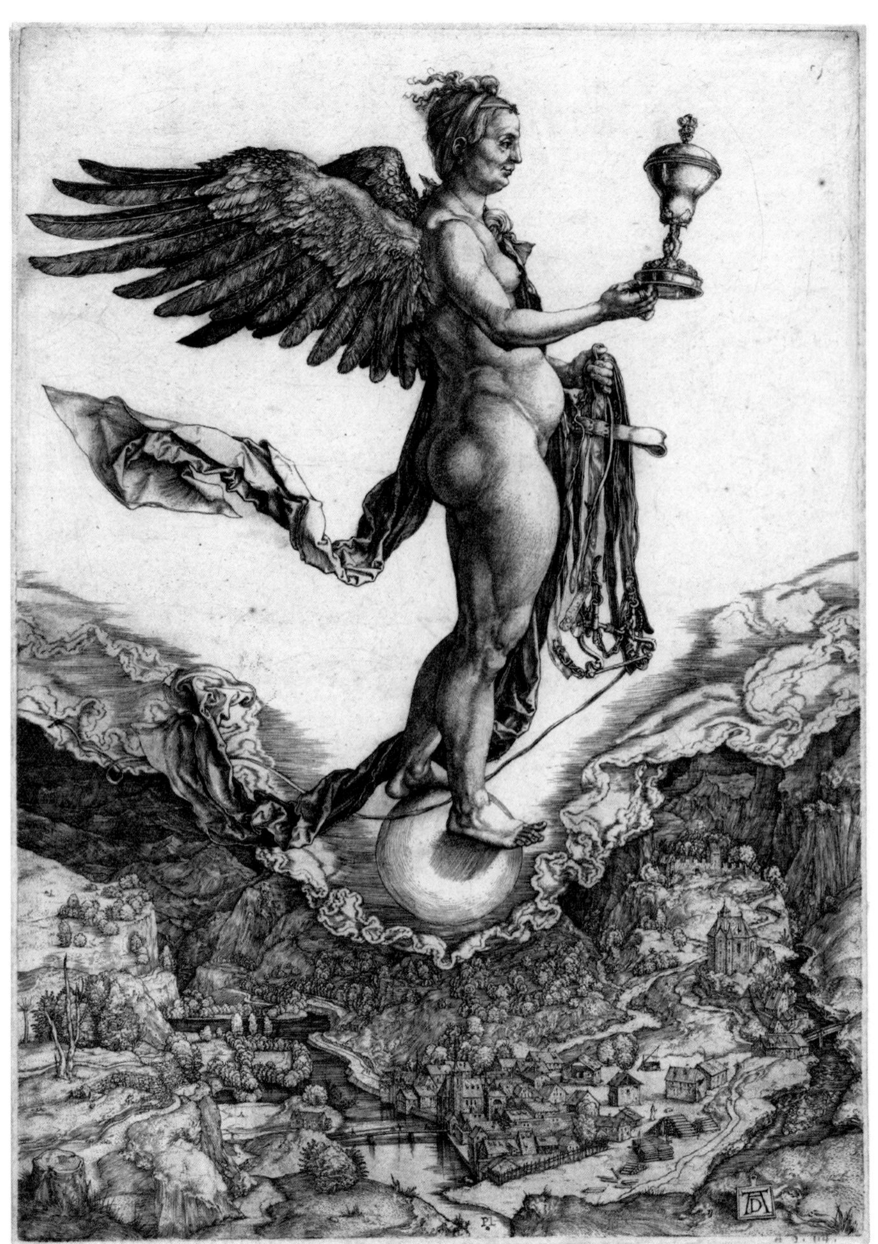

9

ALBRECHT DÜRER

Nemesis (The Large Fortune), C. 1501

Engraving, 329 x 224 mm (plate)

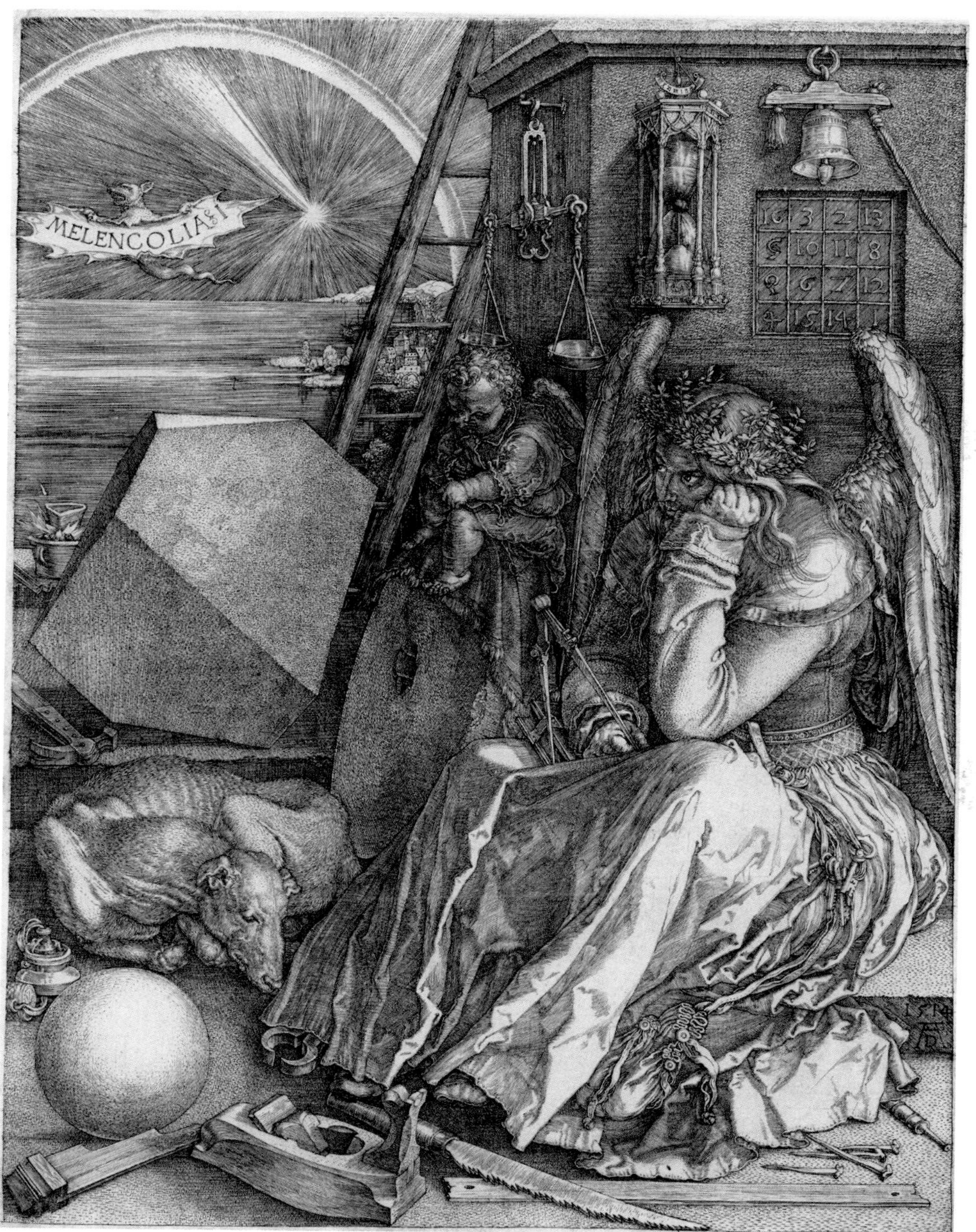

10

ALBRECHT DÜRER

Melencolia I, 1514
Engraving, 239 x 168 mm (plate)

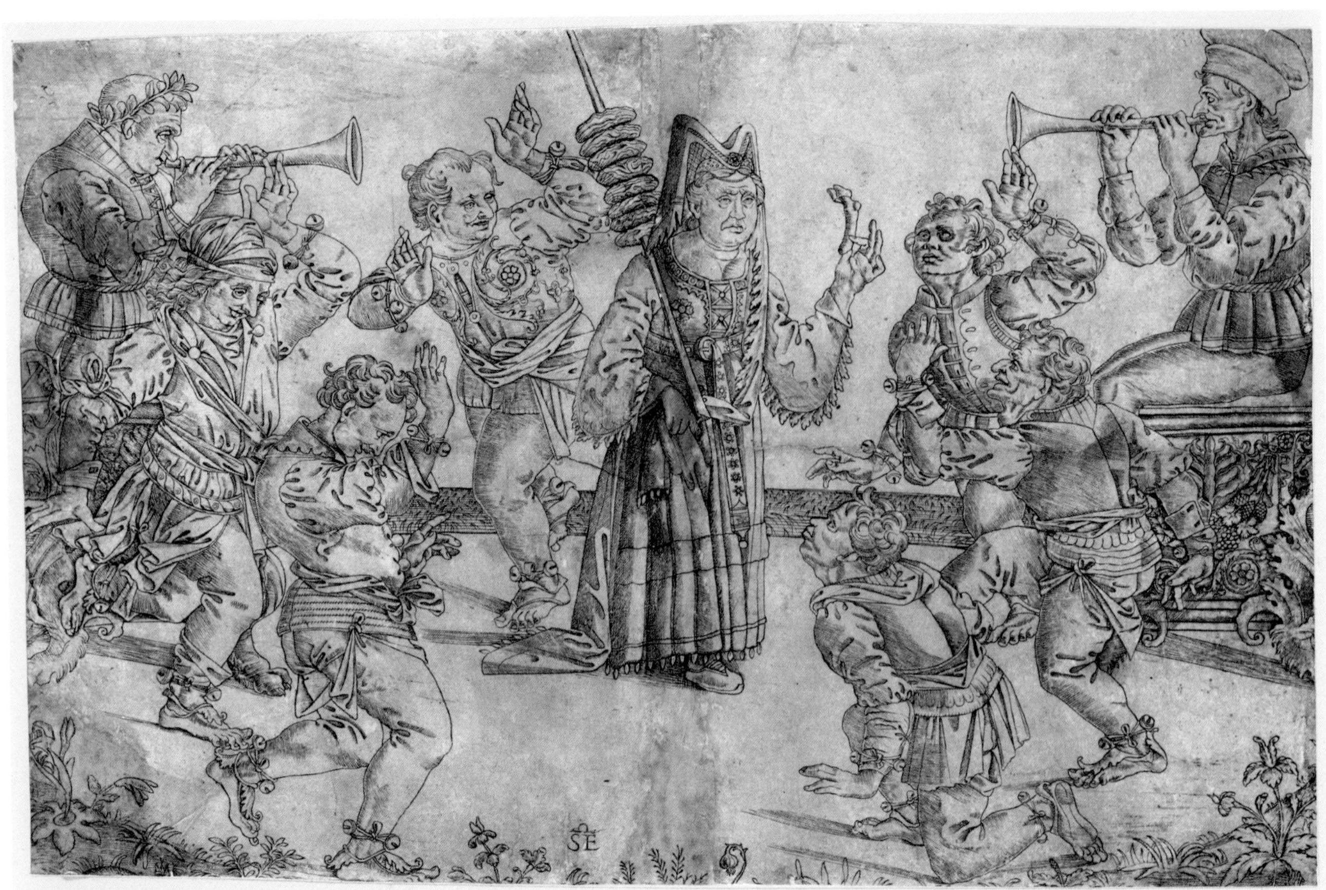

11

Carnival dance ('The Sausage Woman')

Last third of 15th century
Engraving, c. 359 x 554 mm

All the works in the catalogue are from the collections of the Hamburger Kunsthalle. They came to the museum in 1863 from the bequest of Georg Harzen (1790–1863).

1

ALBRECHT DÜRER

Nuremberg 1471–1528 Nuremberg

The Death of Orpheus, 1494

Pen and brown ink, 289 x 225 mm
Dated and monogrammed at centre bottom *1494 A d*;
inscribed on the banderole in the tree: *Orfeus der Erst puseran*
Inv. no. 23006
Winkler 58; Strauss 1494/11

Dürer probably created this drawing at the end of 1494, when he is presumed to have been in Venice (for the question of Dürer's first trip to Italy see Ferrari 2007, pp. 45–49; Eser 2012, pp. 542–44; London 2013, pp. 29–32). The figure of Orpheus is based on an antique representational formula, probably mediated through a lost work by Mantegna. Warburg (1906) interpreted this dependency, for which he developed the term pathos formula (*Pathosformel*), as art historical evidence for Dürer's search for passionate gestures in the art of antiquity. This view contrasted with the traditional supposition, predominant since Winckelmann, that the main characteristic of the art of classical antiquity was the Apollinian formal principle, according to which man was represented in a noble and calm pose.

2

FERRARA

The Death of Orpheus, last third of 15th century

Engraving, 146 x 216 mm
Inv. no. 22
Hind E.III 17

This engraving, which has survived only in this impression, was first identified as a model for Dürer's Orpheus drawing by Charles Ephrussi (1882). While Warburg agreed, Joseph Meder (1911–12) convincingly questioned this on stylistic grounds. The view has since prevailed that both are based on a lost design by Andrea Mantegna. The mark in the centre of the composition has not been identified either as a symbol or as the stamp of a collector, the printer or the artist.

3

ANDREA MANTEGNA

Isola di Carturo near Padua 1431–1506 Mantua

Battle of the sea-gods (left half), c. 1475–80

Engraving and drypoint, 314 x 435 mm (sheet and plate)
Inscribed in the plate on the tablet held by the old woman: *INVID*
[= Invidia]
Inv. no. 63
Bartsch 18; Hind 5

This engraving forms a pair with cat. 4. Richard Förster (1902) associated the subject with the Ichthyophagi, North African coast-dwellers described by Virgil. This view, adopted by Warburg in his lecture (WIA, III, 61.6.1., fol. 35), has been challenged in recent scholarship. Although Erika Simon (1971–72) identifies the *Aeneid* (Book I, 82) as the textual source, Mantegna probably did not illustrate a specific mythological scene but rather created an independent work influenced by sarcophagus reliefs.

4
ANDREA MANTEGNA
Isola di Carturo near Padua 1431–1506 Mantua
Battle of the sea-gods (right half), c. 1475–80

Engraving and drypoint, 305 x 442 mm (sheet and plate)
Inv. no. 63
Bartsch 17; Hind 6

Dürer copied this engraving in a drawing dated 1494, probably made in Venice. The sheet (Albertina, Vienna) is part of a group of four copies after works by Mantegna and Antonio Pollaiuolo which Warburg called 'pathos drawings' (*Pathosblätter*).

5
ANDREA MANTEGNA
Isola di Carturo near Padua 1431–1506 Mantua
Bacchanal with Silenus, c. 1475–80

Engraving and drypoint, 290 x 447 mm (sheet and plate)
Inv. no. 66
Bartsch 30; Hind 3

Like cat. 3–4, this engraving is not a faithful copy after an ancient sarcophagus relief but an independent interpretation of Dionysus's festive procession. Dürer may have copied these engravings by Mantegna during his Italian journey in 1494. For his lecture Warburg borrowed the Mantegna prints as a substitute for these drawings, both of which are in the Albertina in Vienna.

6
ANDREA MANTEGNA
Isola di Carturo near Padua 1431–1506 Mantua
Bacchanal with a wine press, c. 1475–80

Engraving and drypoint, 330 x 457 mm (sheet and plate)
Inv. no. 65
Bartsch 19; Hind 4

In Warburg's loan request to the director of the Kunsthalle, only *Bacchanal with Silenus* is listed. This print may, however, have also been offered to Warburg as a loan, as the numbers "19" and "20", referring to Bartsch's catalogue of Old Master prints, were added to the letter by the museum's staff (doc. 1).

7
ALBRECHT DÜRER
Nuremberg 1471–1528 Nuremberg
Ercules (The Madness of Hercules), c. 1496

Woodcut, 390 x 284 mm (sheet), 390 x 283 mm (block)
Monogrammed in the block bottom right *AD* (ligature);
inscribed in the block on the banderole: *Ercules*
Inv. no. 10856
Bartsch 127; Schoch/Mende/Scherbaum 105

The mythological or allegorical subject depicted here has not yet been identified conclusively (see most recently Schauerte 2012, pp. 208–20). Warburg (1906) used this sheet to argue that Dürer's interest in antiquity focused mainly on its examples of agitated movement. The Fury in the background references the *Battle of the sea-gods* by Mantegna (cat. 3).

8

ALBRECHT DÜRER

Nuremberg 1471–1528 Nuremberg

Hercules at the Crossroads (Jealousy), *c.* 1498

Engraving, 352 x 262 mm (sheet), 323 x 223 mm (plate)
Monogrammed in the plate at bottom centre *AD* (ligature)
Inv. no. 10634
Bartsch 73 (*"L'effet de la jalousie"*); Schoch/Mende/Scherbaum 22

The identification of this scene is not straightforward. According to Erwin Panofsky's interpretation (1930), now widely accepted, it shows the humanist subject of Hercules at the Crossroads, where the protagonist has to choose between the stony path of virtue and the easy path of vice. Dürer referred to the print as 'Hercules' in his Netherlandish diary of 1520–21, without giving any further explanation. For the figures, Dürer drew on his 1494 copies after Mantegna and Pollaiuolo. Warburg (1906) assumed that it represented Zeus and Antiope, and accordingly interpreted the sheet as a classicizing 'temperament image' of human passions.

9

ALBRECHT DÜRER

Nuremberg 1471–1528 Nuremberg

Nemesis (The Large Fortune), *c.* 1501

Engraving, 333 x 233 mm (sheet), 329 x 224 (plate)
Monogrammed in the plate at bottom right *AD* (ligature)
Inv. no. 10638
Bartsch 77; Schoch/Mende/Scherbaum 33

This celebrated engraving, which Dürer entitled *Nemesis* in his Netherlandish diary in 1520–21, is thought to illustrate the 1482 poem *Manto* by the Italian poet Angelo Poliziano (Politian), as first suggested by Karl

Giehlow in 1902. Nemesis was the Greek goddess of retributive justice and as such the personification of revenge. According to Ludwig Justi (1902), Dürer followed the treatise of the classical Roman architect and theorist Vitruvius when defining the figure's proportions. Accordingly, Warburg saw in this work one of the earliest examples of Dürer's interest in a classical canon of forms, which, following Winckelmann, represented the human form tempered and contained rather than passionately agitated.

10

ALBRECHT DÜRER

Nuremberg 1471–1528 Nuremberg

Melencolia I, 1514

Engraving, 244 x 192 mm (sheet), 239 x 168 mm (plate)
Dated and monogrammed in the plate at bottom left *1514 AD* (ligature)
Inv. no. 10635
Bartsch 74; Schoch/Mende/Scherbaum 71

Dürer's *Melencolia I* is one of the most complex allegorical images of all time. Despite countless interpretations it has not been entirely unravelled, as the meaning of the individual attributes of Melancholia may be identified in isolation but remain enigmatic in their interrelation. They do not seem to come together in a coherent system. Thus it remains open whether Dürer understood melancholia as the life-negating temperament of the medieval tradition or whether he interpreted it positively as the fundamental condition of creativity and ingenuity in the humanist sense of the Renaissance (see Schuster 1991). In his Dürer lecture of 1905, Warburg used the print as well as *Nemesis* as

an argument to show that Dürer gradually turned away
from the solemn formal language of Mantegna and
Pollaiuolo after 1500. For Warburg this renunciation of
Italian models did not, however, mean that *Melencolia I*
was a specifically German subject, as its main source is
rooted in the astrology of late Greek-Roman antiquity.

11

FLORENCE

Carnival dance ('The Sausage Woman')

last third of 15th century

Engraving, c. 359 x 554 mm (sheet and plate)
Monogrammed in the plate at bottom centre *S E*
Inv. no. 46a
Hind B.III. 12
Bartsch 74; Schoch/Mende/Scherbaum 71

The monogram $\widehat{SE}$ has traditionally been associated
with the artist Francesco Squarcione from Padua
(*c.* 1394–1468/74). Warburg disputed this attribution.
The exact meaning of the carnivalesque dance scene is
unknown; it presumably stems from Burgundian late
medieval court culture, from whence it came to Italy.
Warburg had originally been planning to borrow this
work for his Dürer lecture of 1905 in order to illustrate
how pagan culture could survive in Western festival
customs. However, shortly before his presentation
Warburg decided not to include the sheet.

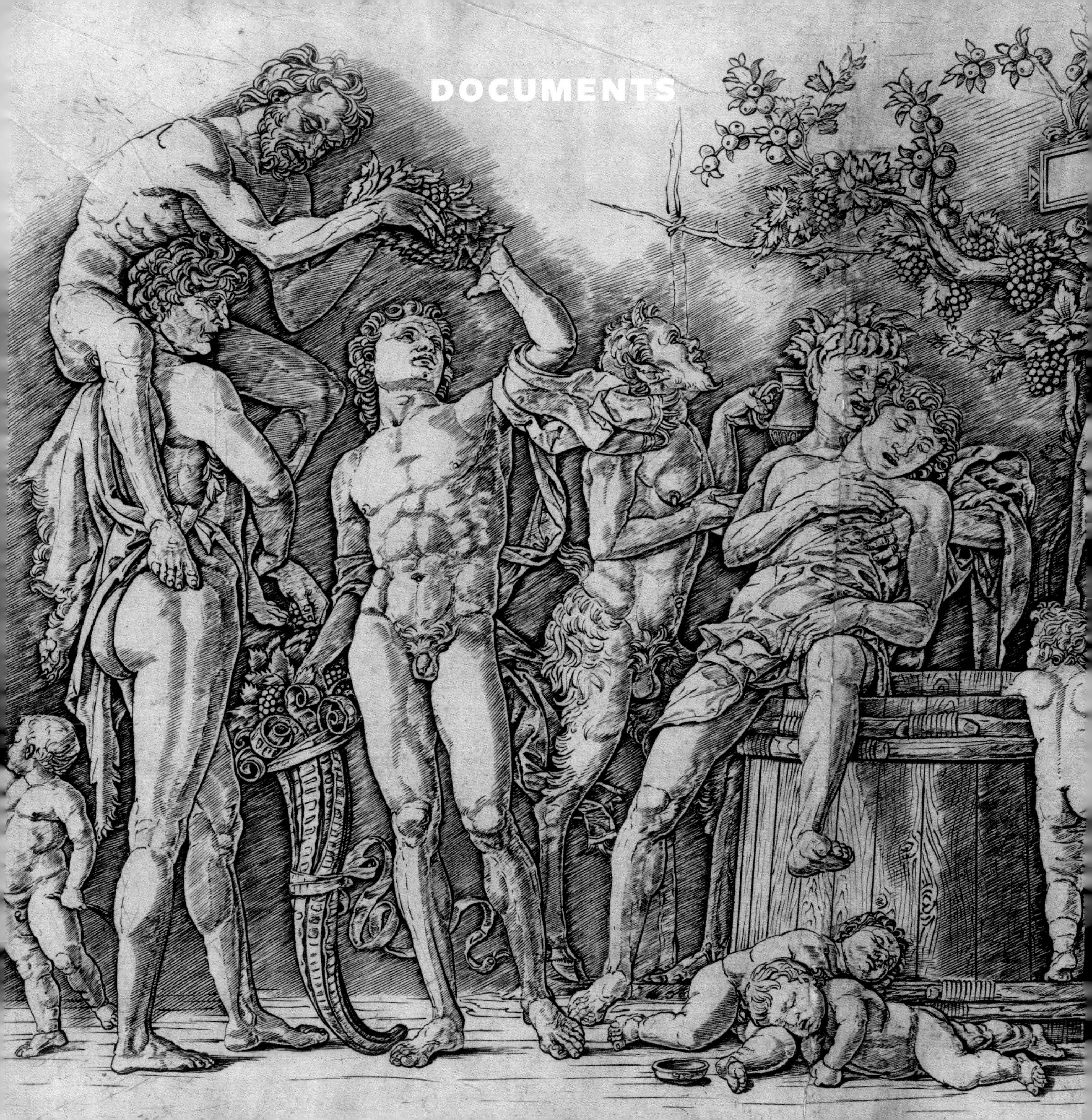

ABBREVIATIONS

HKA   Hamburger Kunsthalle, Archiv
HKB   Hamburger Kunsthalle, Bibliothek
WIA   London, Warburg Institute Archive

DOC. 1

Letter from Aby Warburg to Lichtwark (director
of the hamburger kunsthalle), 1 october 1905
HKA, Direktorenkorrespondenz, no. 73

Hamburg 17/ 52 Benedictstrasse. Tel. IV.1022. [printed
heading]

To the honourable Director Lichtwark: Dear Sir,

I am obliged to you for Bertram and the postcard to the
exhibition [1]; unfortunately tomorrow is folklore day
[2], which would be difficult for me to miss. My lecture
is now scheduled in the combined section, Thursday
between 10:00 and 11:00, and I ask you please to send
your employee at 10:00 with following sheets (to the
'Theatersaal bei Ludwig') [3] [pagebreak]
Dürer, Death of Orpheus, drawing
Death of Orpheus, engraving
Mantegna, Bacchanal with Silenus, B. 19 and 20
Mantegna, Battle of Tritons, B. 15
Mantegna, Sea Centaurs, B. 17 and 18
Dürer, Large Satyr [B.] 69?
Dürer, The Large Fortune, B. 77
Dürer, 'Ercules', B. 127
Dürer, Melencolia I, B. 74 [4]

Yours respectfully, Warburg

[1] The reference is to the exhibition on painting in
Hamburg from the Middle Ages to the nineteenth century,
which opened on 1 October in anticipation of the Congress
of German Philologists.

[2] First congress of the German folklore societies, which
took place in Hamburg, 2 October 1905. Warburg was
involved with the realisation of this event.

[3] This theatre hall, also called Konzerthaus Hamburg, was
managed by the brothers Ludwig.

[4] The numbers written in pencil and starting with the
letter B are in a different hand and are the catalogue
numbers of Adam Bartsch's *Le Peintre Graveur* (1802–21).

Dürer, Tod des Orpheus   [illegible]
S, Tod d. Orpheus   [illegible]

Mantegna, Bacchanal   B. 19 u 20
          mit Silen
Mantegna, [illegible]   B. 15
Mantegna, Seekentauren   B. 17 u 18

Dürer, grosses [illegible]   69 ?
Dürer, grosses [illegible]   B. 77
Dürer, "Ercoles"   B. 127
Dürer, Melancholie   B. 74

          Ihr [illegible]
          [illegible]:
              Warburg

P. H. 1

Hochgeehrter Herr Direktor

          Ich danke Ihnen verbindlichst
durch Bertram für die Karte zur
Ausstellung; leider ist morgen [illegible]-
tag wo ich nur schwer abkommen kann;
Mein Vortrag soll jetzt vor combinirter
[illegible] am Donnerstag zwischen 10 u. 11
[illegible] und ich bitte Sie, mir gefl. um
10 Uhr. Ihren Beamten mit
folgenden Blättern (im [illegible]
bei [illegible]) entgegen zu lassen:

Illustrations accompanying Warburg's 1905 lecture: front leaf ("The death of Orpheus: illustrations for the lecture 'Dürer and Italian Antiquity'. Distributed to the members of the Archaeological Section of the 48th Congress of German Philologist and Teachers in Hamburg, October 1905, by A. Warburg") and plates I, II, III
HKB

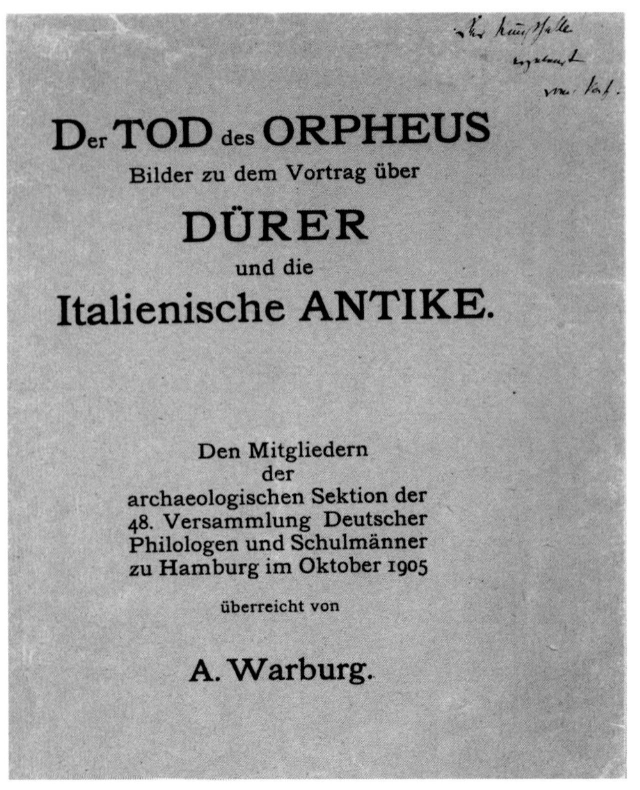

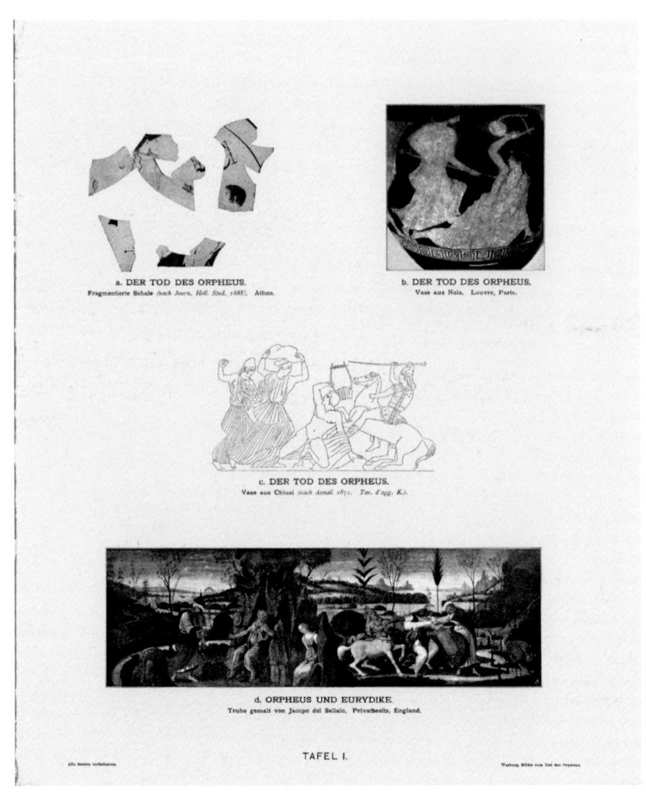

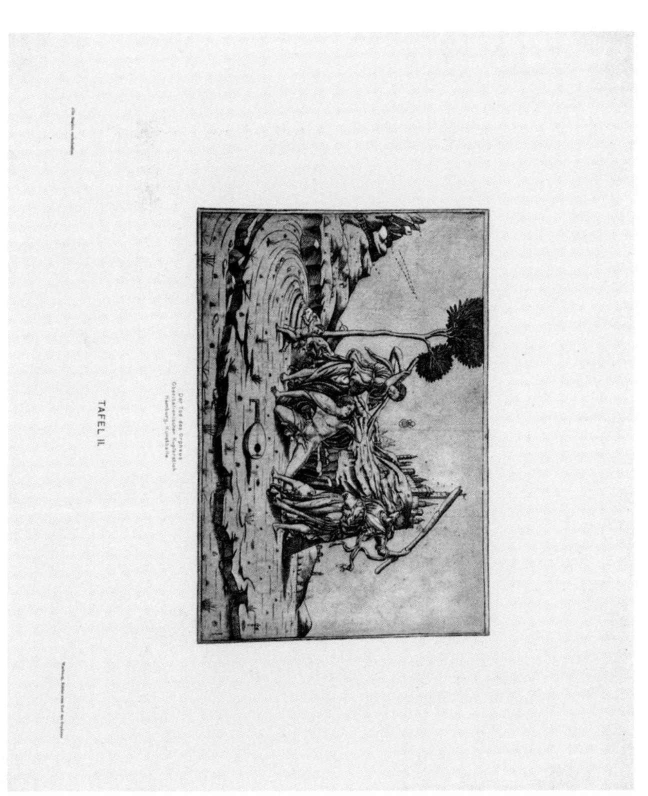

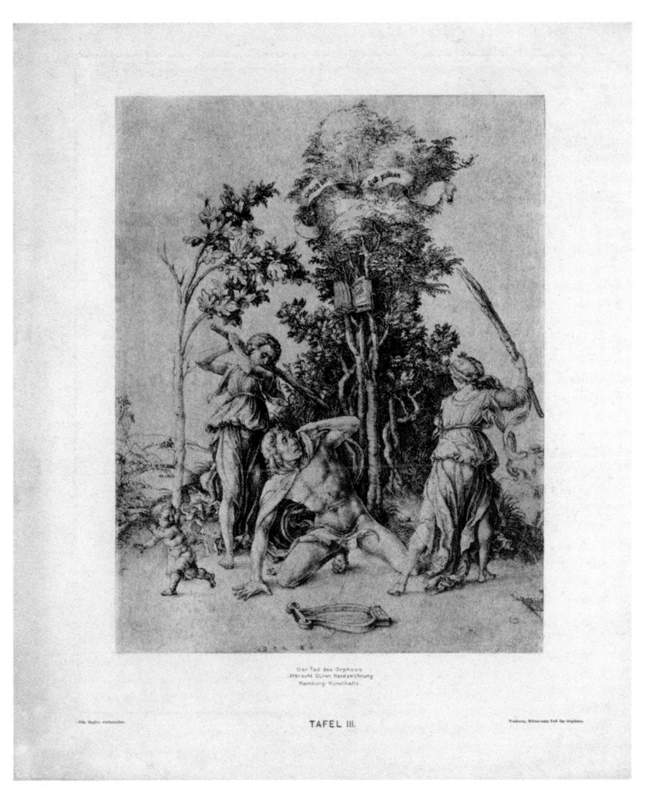

Der Tod des Orpheus
Albrecht Dürer Handzeichnung
Hamburg Kunsthalle

TAFEL III.

Sketch for 'The Death of Orpheus', c. 1905

WIA, III. 61.1., fol. 34

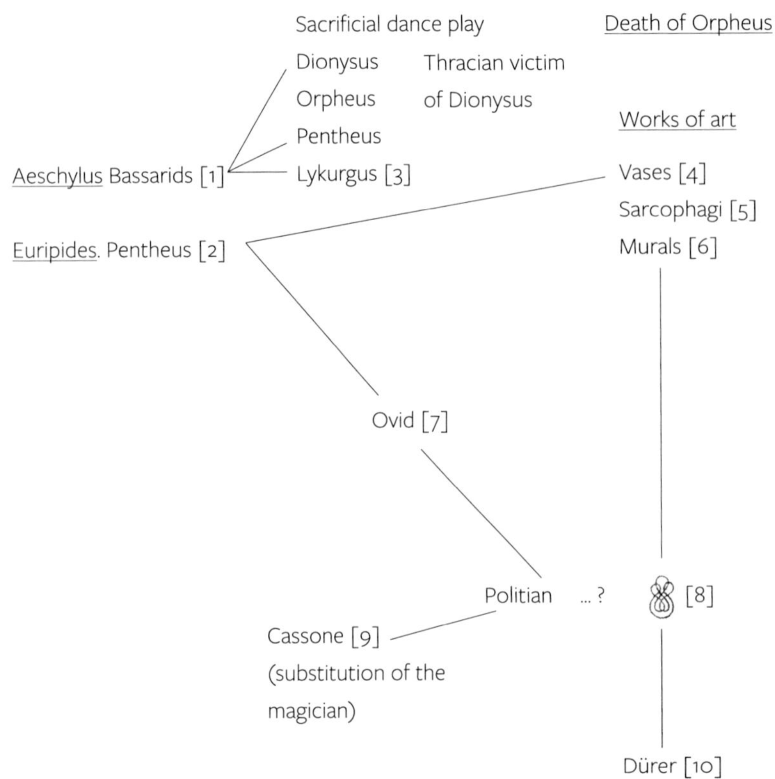

Overview of the literary and pictorial traditions of the
Orpheus myth from classical antiquity to Dürer. Warburg is
concerned above all with the mutual influence of literature
and the visual arts. He presumes that there was a significant
connection between Politian's drama *Fabia di Orfeo* and
the engraving of the death of Orpheus by a Ferrarese
master (cat. 2).

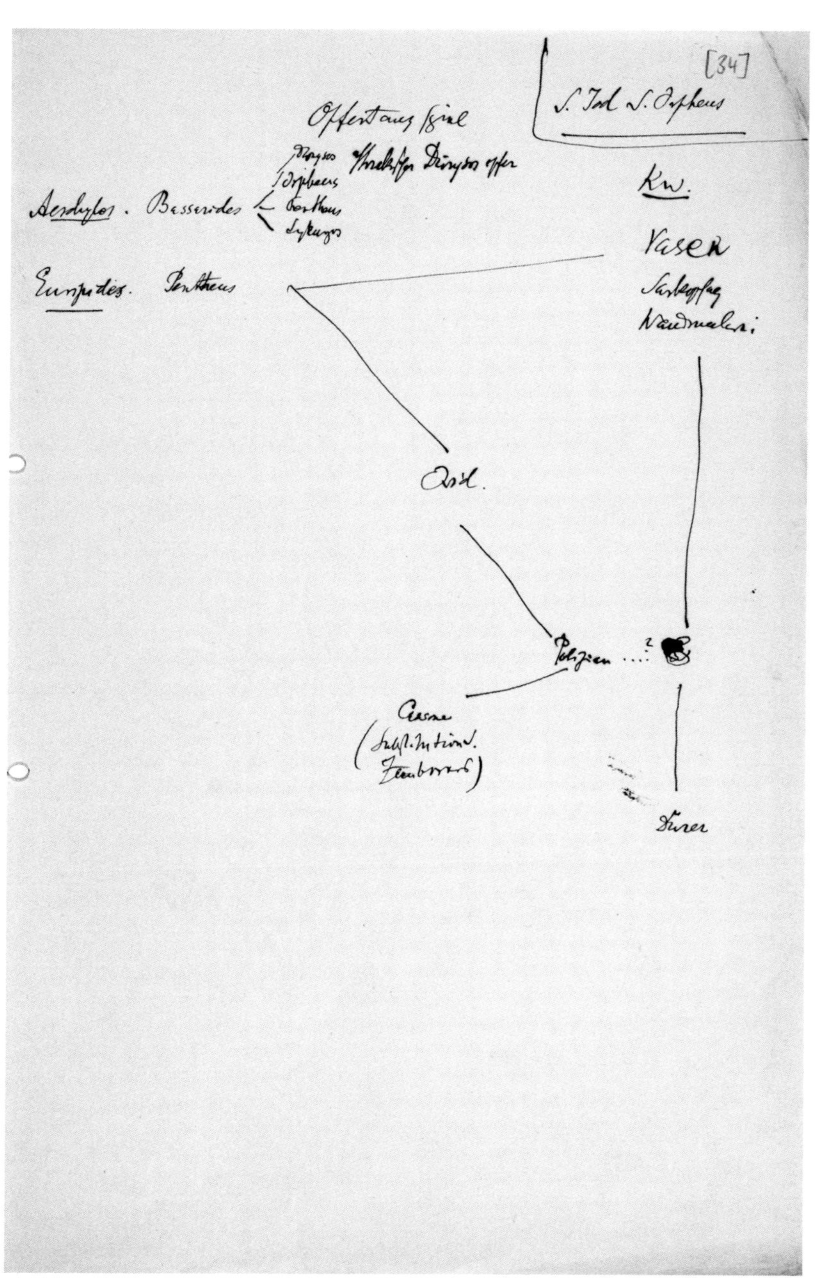
S. Tod d. Orpheus
Offert aus Sizil
Aeschylos . Bassarides
Euripides . Pentheus
Diagras Orpheus Pentheus Lykurgos
Kw.
Vasen
Sarkophag
Wandmalerei
Osd.
Polygnot
Cesare
Dürer

Sketch for 'Dürer and Italian Antiquity', c. 1905

WIA, III. 61.1., fol. 58

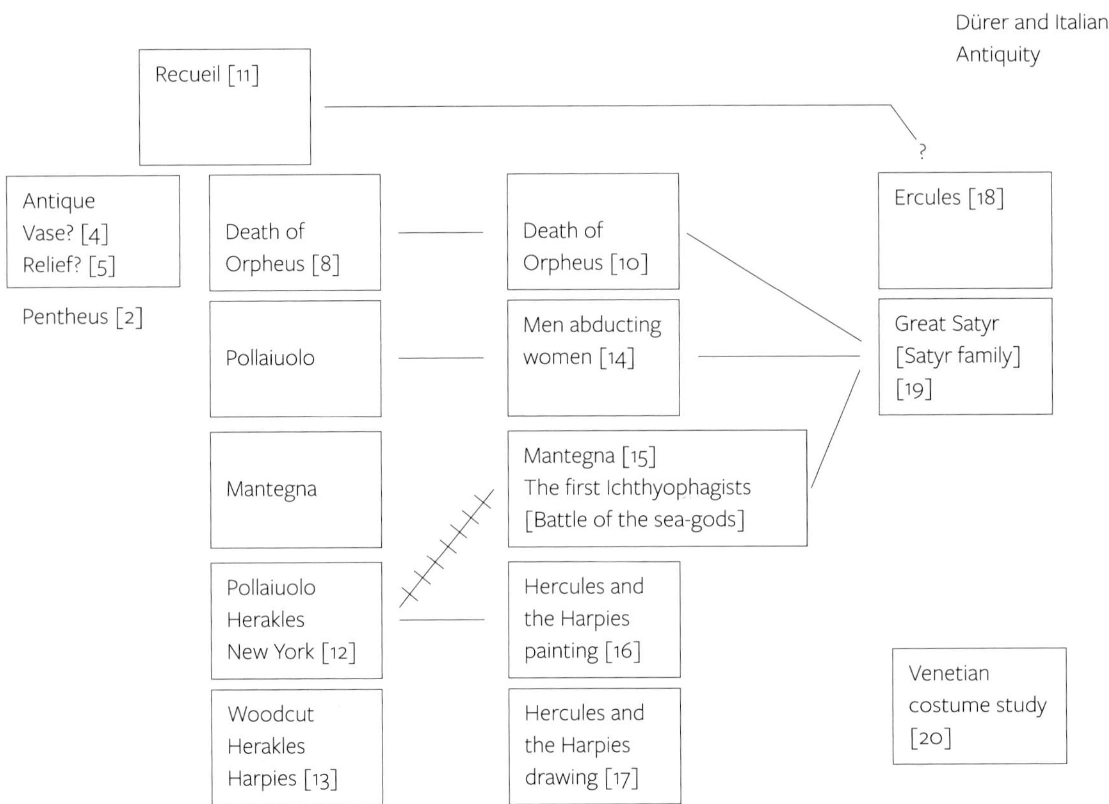

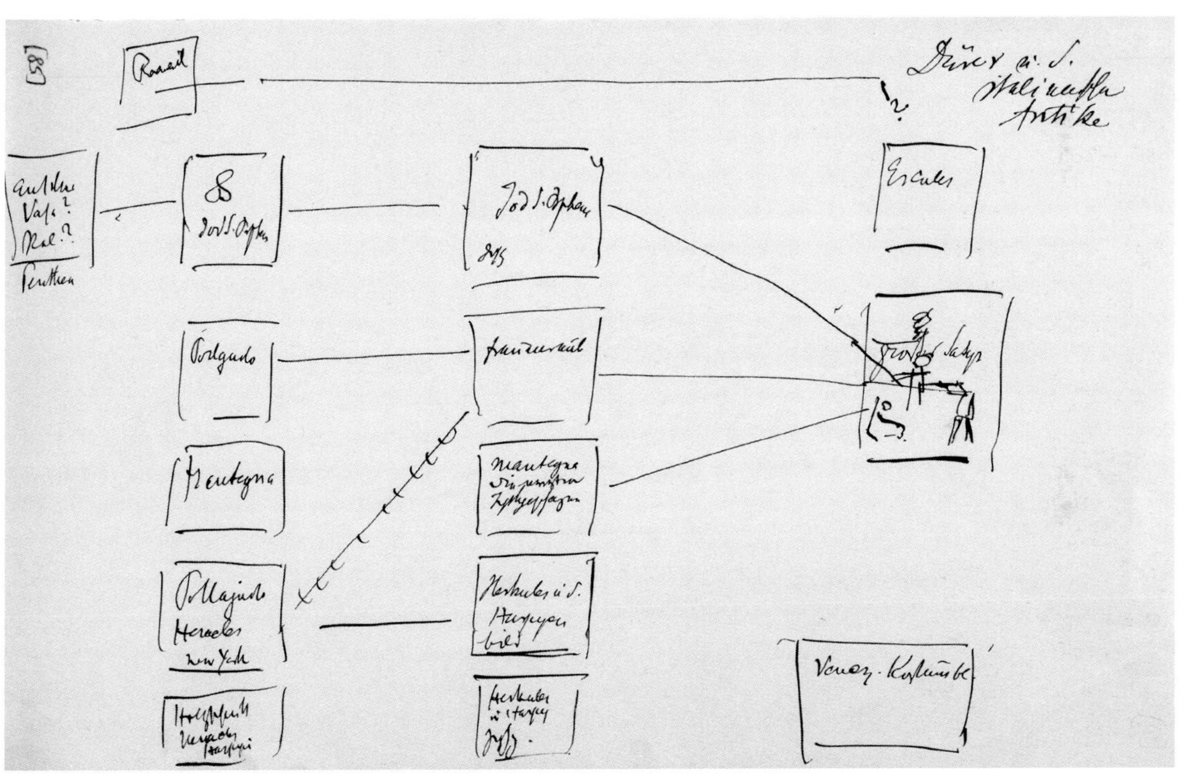

The sketch presents an overview of Dürer's dialogue with classical antiquity. In column 1, classical works of art with representations of the death of Orpheus and Pentheus. In column 2, Italian Renaissance works that influenced Dürer. In column 3, works by Dürer after Mantegna and Pollaiuolo. In column 4, the first independent compositions by Dürer with mythological content, also a Venetian costume study. Warburg's table in its graphic design reminds us of the panels of the picture atlas *Mnemosyne* of the late 1920s (doc. 5; see illustration p. 12).

NOTES

[1] Aeschylus (525–456 BC), Greek tragedian. In his lost drama *The Bassarids*, the subject of Orpheus's murder by the Maenads was treated for the first time.

[2] Euripides (c. 480–406 BC), Greek tragedian. In his drama *The Bacchae*, Pentheus, King of Thebes, was brutally torn to pieces by ecstatic maenads on the order of the god of wine, Dionysus.

[3] In Homer's *Iliad*, Lycurgus, King of Thrace, banished Dionysus from his realm, who, out of revenge, inflicted Lycurgus with a madness like inebriation so that, confusing his son with a grapevine, he killed him. Dionysus further punished the land with barrenness, which ended only with the killing of Lycurgus by his own people or by wild animals from Dionysus's retinue. Warburg recognized the tragic parallels between the Lycurgus and Orpheus myths – Orpheus too was a Thracian king – calling them "Thracian Dionysus victims".

[4] Presumably: fragment of a bowl, National Archaeological Museum, Athens; vase from Nola, Musée du Louvre, Paris; vase from Chiusi, Museo Gregoriano Profano, Vatican; see Warburg 1906, p. 56.

[5] Presumably: sarcophagus, Camposanto Monumentale, Pisa; fragment of a sarcophagus cover, Museo d'Antichità, Turin; see Warburg 1906, p. 56.

[6] Presumably: mural, Domus Vettiorum, Pompeii

[7] Publius Ovidius Naso, called Ovid (20 BC – 17 AD), Roman poet of the imperial era. His epic poem *Metamorphoses* constitutes the most important source for the transmission of ancient pagan myths. The Orpheus myth, including his death, is treated in Books 10 and 11.

[8] See cat. 2.

[9] *Cassone*: Marriage chest typically decorated with mythological or allegorical representations. Presumably the image mentioned in Warburg's slide list (no. 29) and illustrated on *Bildertafel* I to the 1905 Orpheus lecture, that is, *Orpheus and Eurydice* by Jacopo da Sellaio (c. 1441–1493); see Warburg 1906, p. 57.

[10] See cat. 1.

[11] Warburg is probably referring to the *Recueil des histoires de Troie* by Raoul Lefèvre from the second half of the fifteenth century. He suspected that this French courtly romance about the Trojan war which extensively describes Hercules's heroic deeds provided the literary source for

Dürer's woodcut *Ercules* (*The Madness of Hercules*;
cat. 7). Erwin Panofsky was later to interpret this woodcut
as Hercules and Cacus with reference to the French
romance; see Panofsky 1930, pp. 183–84.

[12] Antonio Pollaiuolo, *Hercules and Deianira*, oil on
canvas, transferred from panel, Yale University Art Gallery,
New Haven, CT; see slide list no. 15; see Warburg 1906, p. 58.

[13] Unknown work; not identified by the present author.

[14] Albrecht Dürer, *Men abducting women*, pen and ink,
Musée Bonnat, Bayonne (here fig. 5). After a lost model by
Pollaiuolo; see Warburg 1906, pp. 57–58. .

[15] Albrecht Dürer, *Battle of the sea-gods*, pen and ink,
Albertina, Vienna; see cat. 4.

[16] Albrecht Dürer, *Hercules and the Stymphalian Birds*, oil
on canvas, Germanisches Nationalmuseum, Nuremberg; see
Warburg 1906, p. 58.

[17] Albrecht Dürer, *Hercules and the Stymphalian Birds*,
pen and ink, Hessisches Landesmuseum, Darmstadt; see
slide list no. 13; see Warburg 1906, p. 58.

[18] See cat. 7.

[19] See cat. 8.

[20] Under consideration: *Two Venetian women*, pen and
ink, Albertina, Vienna.

DOC. 5

Aby Warburg, Image table 49 (Dürer) for his picture atlas
Mnemosyne, penultimate version, 2 September 1929
WIA
(See illustration p. 12)

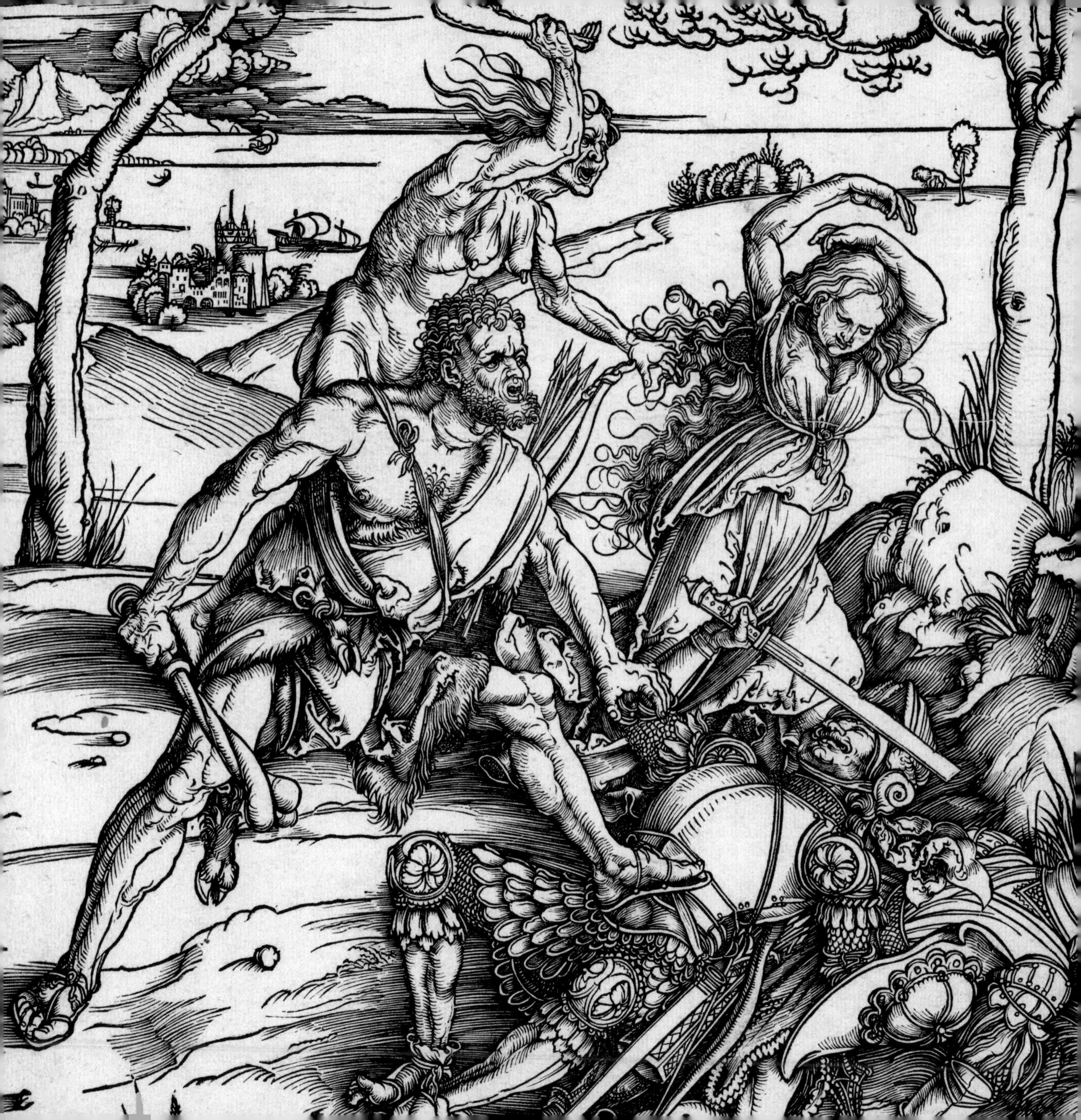

CHRONOLOGY OF WARBURG'S LIFE

1866 Abraham Moritz (Aby) Warburg is born, the eldest son of seven children of a Jewish family of bankers in Hamburg. His father Moritz Warburg (1838–1910) runs the private banking house M.M. Warburg & Co., founded in Altona in 1798.

1873 Enrolment at the Realgymnasium Johanneum, a secondary school in Hamburg.

1879 According to family tradition, the thirteen-year-old Warburg cedes the right of succession of the future management of the bank to his father's second son, Max M. Warburg (1867–1946), on the condition that all his book purchases will be financed throughout his life.

1886 Enrolment at the Friedrich-Wilhelms-Universität in Bonn. Warburg studies art history with Carl Justi and Henry Thode.

1888–89 Warburg is part of a group of students who spend the winter semester in Florence under the supervision of August Schmarsow. Here he develops the idea of writing his doctoral thesis on Sandro Botticelli.

1891 Warburg's dissertation *Sandro Botticellis 'Geburt der Venus' und 'Frühling'* is accepted by the University of Strasbourg.

1893–95 Warburg stays in Florence to undertake further research on Early Renaissance culture and art.

1895–96 On the occasion of the wedding of his brother Paul M. Warburg (1868–1932), Warburg travels to New York. Afterwards he goes on a long research trip to the Indian reservations in the western United States of America.

1897 Warburg marries the painter and sculptor Mary Hertz (1866–1934), whom he had met in Florence in 1888. They go on to have three children together.

1900 In August, Warburg rejects an offer by Alfred Lichtwark to become Museum Assistant at the Hamburger Kunsthalle. As a counter-proposal, Warburg offers to work on the Old Master holdings of the Print Room as an independent scholar and publish his research in a catalogue of the collection. Lichtwark rejects this project for financial and administrative reasons.

1900–03 In agreement with his brother, Max M. Warburg, Warburg plans for the foundations of a library for cultural studies in Hamburg and starts to acquire books systematically.

1904 Warburg returns with his family from Florence to Hamburg.

1906 Warburg rejects the offer of a professorship at the University of Breslau.

1909 Purchase of a city mansion on Heilwigweg 114 in Hamburg.

1912 Warburg rejects the offer to become the successor of Professor Adolph Goldschmidt at the University of Halle; he receives an honorary professorship from the Hamburg Senate.

From 1913 Warburg becomes a lecturer for holiday courses in Hamburg.

1914 The Viennese art historian Fritz Saxl, who has been in contact with Warburg since 1910–11, becomes a research assistant at the Warburg library.

1918–24 Owing to his mental health, which has worsened during the First World War, Warburg has to stay at psychiatric hospitals. In spring 1921, Warburg admits himself to a sanatorium in Kreuzlingen on Lake Constance, which is run by Dr. Ludwig Binswanger. Warburg is diagnosed first with schizophrenia and then with severe depression. On 12 August 1924, Warburg is released from the sanatorium as cured.

1925–26 Construction of the Warburg Library for Cultural Studies on the land neighbouring the family's estate on Heilwigstrasse (opening 1 May 1926).

1925–29 Warburg becomes a private lecturer at the Art History Institute of the University of Hamburg. From c. 1926 he works on the picture atlas *Mnemosyne*. It is Warburg's last, and unfinished, research project on the heritage of the ancient world of the gods in Western art.

1929 Warburg dies on 26 October of a heart attack. He is buried in the main cemetery in Ohlsdorf.

SELECTED LITERATURE

WARBURG'S WRITINGS AND
COLLECTIONS OF ESSAYS

WARBURG 1906
Aby Warburg, *Dürer und die italienische Antike. Sonder-Abdruck aus den Verhandlungen der 48. Versammlung deutscher Philologen und Schulmänner zu Hamburg im Okt. 1905*, Leipzig, 1906

WARBURG 1932/1998
Aby Warburg, *Gesammelte Schriften*, vol. I: *Die Erneuerung der heidnischen Antike. Kulturwissenschaftliche Beiträge zur Geschichte der europäischen Renaissance. Mit einem Anhang unveröfffentlicher Schriften*, 2 vols., ed. Gertrud Bing in collaboration with Fritz Rougemont, Leipzig 1932; newly edited by Horst Bredekamp and Michael Diers, Berlin, 1998

WARBURG 1979
Aby Warburg, *Ausgewählte Schriften und Würdigungen*, ed. by Dieter Wuttke in collaboration with Carl Georg Heise, Baden-Baden, 1979

WARBURG 2000
Aby Warburg, *Gesammelte Schriften*, vol. II: 1: *Der Bilderatlas Mnemosyne*, ed. Martin Warnke in collaboration with Claudia Brink, Berlin, 2000

WARBURG 2010
Aby Warburg, *Werke in einem Band. Auf der Grundlage der Manuskripte und Handexemplare*, ed. with commentary by Martin Treml, Sigrid Weigel and Perdita Ludwig, Berlin, 2010

SECONDARY LITERATURE

BARTSCH
Adam Bartsch, *Le Peintre Graveur*, 21 vols., Vienna, 1802–21

BIAŁOSTOCKI 1986
Jan Białostocki, *Dürer and his Critics, 1500–1971: Chapters in the history of ideas, including a collection of texts*, Baden-Baden, 1986

BURCKHARDT 1860
Jacob Burckhardt, *Die Cultur der Renaissance in Italien. Ein Versuch*, Basle, 1860

BURCKHARDT [1990]
Jacob Burckhardt, *The Civilisation of the Renaissance in Italy*, trans S.G.C. Middlemore, London, 1990

DIDI-HUBERMAN 2002
Georges Didi-Huberman, *L'image survivante: histoire de l'art et temps des fantômes selon Aby Warburg*, Paris, 2002

EPHRUSSI 1882
Charles Ephrussi, *Dürer Dessins*, Paris, 1882

EKSERDJIAN 1998
David Ekserdjian, 'Mantegna's lost Death of Orpheus', in Wolfgang Liebenwein and Anchise Tempestini (eds.), *Gedenkschrift für Richard Harprath*, Berlin, 1998, pp. 145–50

ESER 2012
Thomas Eser, 'Materialien für eine Dürer-Matrix von 1471 bis 1505', in Daniel Hess and Thomas Eser (eds.), *Der frühe Dürer*, exh. cat., Germanisches Nationalmuseum, Nuremberg 2012, pp. 536–52

FERRARI 2007
Simone Ferrari, 'Dürer e il veneto', in Kristina Herrmann Fiore (ed.), *Dürer e l'Italia*, exh. cat., Scuderie del Quirinale, Rome 2007, pp. 45–49

FÖRSTER 1902
Richard Förster, 'Die Meergötter des Mantegna', *Jahrbuch der Königlich Preussischen Kunstsammlungen*, vol. 23, 1902, pp. 205–15

GIEHLOW 1902
Carl Giehlow, 'Poliziano und Dürer', *Die Graphischen Künste. Gesellschaft für vervielfältigende Kunst*, vol. 25, 1902, no. 2, pp. 25–26

GOMBRICH 1970
Ernst H. Gombrich, *Aby Warburg. An Intellectual Biography. With a Memoir on the History of the Library by Fritz Saxl*, London, 1970

GUTHMÜLLER 1986
Bodo Guthmüller, *Studien zur antiken Mythologie in der italienischen Renaissance*, Weinheim, 1986

HIND
Arthur M. Hind, *Early Italian Engraving. A critical catalogue with complete reproduction of all the prints described*, 7 vols., London, 1938–48

HOFMANN/SYAMKEN/WARNKE 1980
Werner Hofmann, Georg Syamken and Martin Warnke, *Die Menschenrechte des Auges. Über Aby Warburg*, ed. Henning Ritter, Frankfurt am Main, 1980

HURTTIG 2011
Marcus Andrew Hurttig, *Die entfesselte Antike. Aby Warburg und die Geburt der Pathosformel in Hamburg*, exh. cat., Hamburger Kunsthalle, 2011

JUSTI 1902
Ludwig Justi, *Konstruierte Figuren und Köpfe unter den Werken Albrecht Dürers. Untersuchungen und Rekonstruktionen*, Leipzig, 1902

LONDON 2013
Stephanie Buck and Stephanie Porras (eds.), *The Young Dürer. Drawing the Figure*, exh. cat., The Courtauld Gallery, London, 2013

MEDER 1911–12
Joseph Meder, 'Neue Beiträge zur Dürer-Forschung', *Jahrbuch der Kunsthistorischen Sammlungen des Allerhöchsten Kaiserhauses*, vol. 30, 1911–12, no. 4, pp. 183–222

NIETZSCHE [1964]
Friedrich Nietzsche, *Complete Works*, ed. by Oscar Levy, 18 vols., New York, 1964, vol. 1: *The Birth of Tragedy or Hellenism and Pessimism*, trans. William August Haussmann

NIETZSCHE [1999]
Friedrich Nietzsche, *Sämtliche Werke. Kritische Studienausgabe*, ed. Giorgio Colli and Mazzino Montinari, 15 vols., Munich, 1999, vol. 1: *Die Geburt der Tragödie oder Griechentum und Pessimismus*

PANOFSKY 1930
Erwin Panofsky, *Hercules am Scheideweg und andere antike Bildstoffe in der neueren Kunst*, Leipzig and Berlin, 1930

PIRROTTA 1975
Nino Pirrotta, *Li due Orfei: da Poliziano a Monteverdi*, revised edn Turin 1975

PRANGE 2007
Peter Prange, *Deutsche Zeichnungen. 1450–1800*, 2 vols., in Hubertus Gaßner and Andreas Stolzenburg (eds.), *Die Sammlungen der Hamburger Kunsthalle, Kupferstichkabinett*, Hamburg, 2007

ROESLER-FRIEDENTHAL 1996
Antoinette Roesler-Friedenthal, 'Ein Porträt Andrea Mantegnas als alter "Orpheus" im Kontext seiner Selbstdarstellungen', *Römisches Jahrbuch der Bibliotheca Hertziana*, vol. 31, 1996, pp. 149–86

RUSSELL 2007
Mark A. Russell, *Between Tradition and Modernity. Aby Warburg and the Public Purposes of Art in Hamburg, 1896–1918*, New York and Oxford, 2007

SCHAUERTE 2012
Thomas Schauerte, 'Peripeteia. Konrad Celtis, die Nürnberger Poetenschule und Dürers "Ercules"', in Daniel Hess and Thomas Eser (eds.), *Der frühe Dürer*, exh. cat., Germanisches Nationalmuseum, Nuremberg, 2012, pp. 208–20

SCHOCH/MENDE/SCHERBAUM
Rainer Schoch, Matthias Mende, Anna Scherbaum, *Albrecht Dürer. Das druckgraphische Werk*, 3 vols., Munich, London and New York, 2001–04

SCHOELL-GLASS 2008
Charlotte Schoell-Glass, *Aby Warburg and Anti-Semitism. Political Perspective on Image and Culture*, trans. Samuel Pakucs Willcocks, Detroit, 2008

SCHRÖTER 2003
Elisabeth Schröter, 'Orpheus in der Kunst des Mittelalters und der Renaissance. Eine Vorläufige Untersuchung', in Christine Mundt-Éspin (ed.), *Blick auf Orpheus. 2500 Jahre europäischer Rezeptionsgeschichte eines antiken Mythos*, Tübingen and Basle, 2003, pp. 109–58

SCHUSTER 1991
Klaus-Peter Schuster, *Melencolia I. Dürers Denkbild*, 2 vols., Berlin, 1991

SETTIS 1993
Salvatore Settis, 'Kunstgeschichte als vergleichende Kulturwissenschaft: Aby Warburg, die Pueblo-Indianer und das Nachleben der Antike', in Thomas Gaehtgens (ed.), *Künstlerischer Austausch. Artistic Exchange. Akten des XXVIII. Internationalen Kongresses für Kunstgeschichte. Berlin, 15.–20. Juli 1992*, 3 vols., Berlin, 1993, vol. 1, pp. 139–58

SIMON 1971–72
Erika Simon, 'Dürer und Mantegna', *Anzeiger des Germanischen Nationalmuseums*, 1971–72, pp. 21–40

STRAUSS 1974
Walter L. Strauss, *The Complete Drawings of Albrecht Dürer*, 6 vols., New York, 1974

WARDEN 1982
John Warden (ed.), *Orpheus. The Metamorphoses of a Myth*, Toronto and elsewhere, 1982

WEISBACH 1906
Werner Weisbach, *Der junge Dürer. Drei Studien*, Leipzig, 1906

WINCKELMANN 1825–29
Joseph Eiselein (ed.), *Johann Winckelmanns sämtliche Werke*, 12 vols., Donauöschingen, 1825–29

WINCKELMANN [1987]
Johann Joachim Winckelmann, *Reflections on the Imitation of Greek Works in Painting and Sculpture*, trans. Elfriede Heyer and Roger C. Norton, La Salle, 1987

WINCKELMANN [2006]
Johann Joachim Winckelmann, *History of the Art of Antiquity*, introduction by Alex Potts, trans. Harry Francis Mallgrave, Los Angeles, 2006

WIND 1991
Edgar Wind, 'Warburgs Begriff der Kulturwissenschaft und seine Bedeutung für die Ästhetik', in *Aby Warburg. Von Michelangelo bis zu den Puebloindianern*, ed. Kulturforum Warburg (Warburger Schriften, vol. 5), Paderborn 1991, pp. 57–78

WINKLER 1936–39
Friedrich Winkler, *Die Zeichnungen Albrecht Dürers*, 4 vols., Berlin, 1936–39